One Teacher's Alphabet:

Ruminations on Learning

Judith M. Meloy

One Teacher's Alphabet: Ruminations on Learning
©2020 by Judith M. Meloy

Cover Design ©2020 by Debbi Wraga

ISBN: 978-1-60571-522-3

Printed in the United States of America

Dedication

With sincere respect and loyal affection, I dedicate this book to Dr. Michelle "Shelly" Contreras, the first person I met at Indiana University where each of us would begin our doctoral studies in the late summer of 1983. Shelly struck me as being simultaneously a most tender and courageous soul, which her life before and since has proven to be the case. As an elementary teacher, Shelly wanted to become a principal in order to affect change more significantly. Upon earning her doctorate, she held several leadership positions, including being the lead learner and shepherd of what was to become recognized as a national Blue Ribbon School.

I was and still am so very proud of this smart, talented, and humble woman. I believe she would agree that even when we stop teaching, when we stop being the educators we so loved being, we *don't* stop thinking about the time we spent, the young people who stole our hearts, and the colleagues who also believed.

Shelly, this small volume is some of what I have been thinking about during the years we have been apart. Thank you for the inspiration.

Preface: Then and Now

I have been contemplating and completing my ABCs for more than 25 years. I constructed two Tables of Content, the first of which introduces the letter and concept I chose to write about, A is for Attitude, and so on. The first alphabet represents my initial writing and thinking, which includes reflections about my first years of teaching during the late 1970s and early 1980s. You will notice these ABCs were written between the years of 1994 and 1997, while I was a relatively new professor at Castleton State College in Vermont. Teaching undergraduate and graduate college students was different than my experiences with middle and high school students might have led me to expect. As I pondered my current setting and students in relationship to that learning, I needed to write my thinking down in order to see what I was trying to understand. Soon, the first alphabet in this book was finished. I know I shared it with one or two of my students in a miniature-sized document, so it would not overwhelm. Sue Woods? Scott Waller? Maybe.

On and off for the next 15 years or so, I learned ever more about thinking, learning, and teaching from my students. Taking early retirement did not stop my teaching, which only ended three years ago with the cessation of what had been a four-year opportunity to work with incoming transfer students (not *their* favorite thing to do at 8 a.m. in the morning, for sure!). Since 2006, and with the acquisition of yet another new computer to get up and running, I came across the old pages, the first edition. As I read, I wondered if maybe I hadn't changed at all; the words still sounded like me. I recognized the learning moments as ones that retain a certain consequence.

Additionally, I awoke one morning to realize that my alphabet would probably be different were I writing it today. And so, to test the thought, I reconsidered my choices and have ever since supplemented many of the letters with an additional concept or more recent thinking. That alphabet is located in *the second* Table of Contents. In the text itself, you will notice I update the original concept immediately below, although in a smaller font. These sections are also indicated with the more recent date and title.

I hope you will remember my thinking exists within the context of time and experience. I did not edit my thoughts in the first alphabet at all, although in more than several places it was very tempting to do so! It is clear, as you will read – and perhaps smile about – I was still learning.

Feel free to wander around the ABCs in any order that strikes you, because that most accurately describes how I wrote them. It is true, however, letter A was the first learning story I wanted to clarify, and it remains among my favorite of the letters in the book. Although ideas intertwine across the alphabet, each letter is meant to stand alone. So, get comfy and pick a letter! Find what interests you and go from there; this is *not* a text!

Yours sincerely,

Judy Meloy, aka "Dr. Meloy/Dr. J"
and once upon a time in a land far away,
"Frau Koonts" 😊

Table of Contents

1994 – 1997

A	Attitude	1
B	Believe	7
C	Curiosity	11
D	Delight	15
E	Energy	19
F	Fun = Work = Learning (F = W = L)	23
G	Grace	25
H	Harmony	27
I	Intellect	31
J	Jump (courage)	35
K	Knowledge	41
L	Living, Loving, Learning, Laughing, Listening	43
M	Meaning	45
N	Notice	47
O	Opportunity	51

P	Power	53
Q	Quit	57
R	Recognition	61
S	Sympathy	63
T	Trust	65
U & V	Understanding and Validity	69
W	Work = Learning = Fun	71
X	Marks the Spot!	73
Y	Yes!	77
Z	Zazz!	81
References		83

Table of Contents

1998 – 2020

A	Awake!	5
B	Believe?	9
C	Caring	13
D	Delight!	17
E	Economize!	20
F	The Challenge (of F = W = L)	23
G	Grace	26
H	Hypothesize	28
I	Hypothesize!	33
J	Juxtapose!	40
K	Knowledge, continued	41
L	The 5 Ls	43
M	Magnanimity	46
N	Narrate	47
O	Ordinary	51
P	Power	55
Q	Query	58

R	Recognize!	62
S	Sharing	64
T	Trust, revisited	67
U & V	Understanding and Validity	69
W	PS	71
X	Wanting Time	74
Y	Yes (continued)	79
Z	I still believe	81
References		83

Introduction

The Covid Spring of 2020 has created a direct challenge to teaching and learning. What we might have imagined as a futuristic scenario *is* the "new normal." Teachers are meeting their students through a screen, trying to encourage reading or art, trying to instruct mathematics or science. Teachers are trying to reach children and young adults who learn best among others, "hands-on." As a result, teachers are rethinking what succeeds and what doesn't, when, and why; they are relying on old instincts and testing new ideas. The opportunities and challenges of teaching have never been more obvious, just as caring and careful teaching have never been more needed. Teachers, each and all of you, are surely feeling this weight.

In the Fall of 1997, I found *I* was needing inspiration and support for the best I could do and be. I knew I believed strongly in the potential of every human being, every person to whom the word "student" or "learner" might be applied. I decided to pull together some of my thoughts, in order to reaffirm my belief in the profession I had chosen. I committed myself to the hope in my heart. I decided we can all be better than we are, in part simply by believing being better is something to strive for, daily, rather than as a "best" offered as a fait de accompli.

In 2020, this attempt may seem a bit 'pollyanna-ish.' However, *the one thing we have in common* is the occupation of teaching and learning. We learn by doing. We learn both the structure and organization of teaching even as we learn other, more subtle aspects of the work. The explication of this latter learning forms the basis of my "alphabet" and the post 1994 - 1997 updates to it.

When I was in graduate school, I thought of myself as the "A-" girl. I had it in me to get solid As, but that was not the goal. I knew it was the funky earrings, the socks that didn't quite match, the fun hats, and a view of the world through rose-colored glasses who were really me, the not-quite-perfect and the not-caring-to-be-so woman, *no grade attached*. I had learned that no matter what we think of ourselves, others will 'grade' us, judge us, and choose other than us. Remembering all of that, I wrote this book for me. Now, in this spring of COVID19, I have decided to share it with you because it is our capacity *to learn* that enables us to be the teachers our students need. Maybe something I went through or thought about will be of value to you during difficult days.

The ABCs detailed here lay bare my thinking and reasoning related to what were, in more than several cases, fundamental and pivotal shifts in my learning about teaching, which began in 1975, several years after returning to school to earn my license. The alphabet attempts to ferret out, make explicit, and honor the "invisible" thinking and decision making embedded in our profession because I have never been sure that our thinking and the 'pre'/'post' lesson planning we do are fully grasped by those not *in* this profession. We interact with human lives, minds, hearts, spirits, bodies. Every day. There is little we accomplish that *doesn't* require our thinking and consideration. Every day. Change is a constant for us. Every day. Although teaching is a complex, and recently, an overtly "appreciated" profession, I continue to believe it is the mental aspects of our work that make it a *highly underrated* one.

I hope you-all are talking with each other, sharing your successes and frustrations. Fall 2020 is *your* fall, as will be all the ones to follow. I will not wish the "force" to be with you. I wish this book to encourage the force *within* you.

Acknowledgements

In this space, way too small, I will be brief (about the only place *in* this book!). I remember you, teachers of mine, former students and colleagues, across grade levels, state boundaries, and decades. You have enriched my life, challenged my "knowing," and shared time with me. You have touched my life and reside in the best work I have done. Because of you, I kept trying and aspiring to be my best. You deserved those attempts, those efforts, and I am grateful for you. With you, my life has never been boring! Thank you.

1994

| A | **Awareness** of Attitudes and Assumptions

I can remember my father remanding me, "It's not *what* you said, it's *how* you said it!" or my mother saying, "I *love* you, it's your *attitude* I don't like." Fight it as I might, when I thought about what they were saying, I do remember realizing this invisible thing (at least to me) called "attitude" was often quite clear to others. As I grew older, I thought my words and attitude had come together, most likely because they were no longer being called to my attention.

Then, in the fall of 1976, I was hired to teach middle school German in Ohio's Centerville City School district. My opportunity came as the result of a maternity leave; I was quite excited to have the chance to teach full-time. German positions were rare. I had been substituting and waitressing for two years.

Upon receiving the list of topics the 8th graders needed to learn during the spring of the year, I quickly saw most of the "fun" topics (culture, food, music, history, geography, etc.) had been "covered." The "to do" list for me included the past tense, modals (helping verbs), word order after "dass" clauses, etc. In other words, my job was to focus on the grammar aspects of middle school foreign language instruction. "Fortunately," I thought, "that's good for me." I had studied German in high school and college; I took matters like correct spelling and word order quite seriously. German is a serious language!

After about 6 weeks, however, I was terribly frustrated. I had 6th graders who could not spell their own names correctly, let alone the German articles for "a/an" or "the." In the 7th grade, more than several students were unable to tell a noun from a verb in English; distinguishing nouns that were subjects from nouns that were direct objects was a new challenge, and some of the 8th graders were taller than I! I headed to the principal's office with my first two concerns. Some of these students simply shouldn't *be* in my classes, I thought; they were weak students and would not be able to achieve a passing grade. "Why," I asked, "does this district set them up for *failure*?"

Carl Berg, the principal, listened to me and smiled as if he knew a great secret. He shared the philosophy of the district. He told me it offered a middle school foreign language program to all students because a portion of the kids would be unable to register for a foreign language class by the time they reached high school. By the 9th grade, these kids would be signing up for double periods of reading or math, or getting extra help from the resource room. The district's philosophy stated all children should have the opportunity to be exposed to a foreign culture, "even if they only remember a couple of words or phrases. Your job, Judy, is to make sure the experience is a successful one for every student." I walked out of his office, still concerned. How could I hold on to *my* beliefs about the value of learning German correctly and *not* flunk some students? Although I was quite impressed with the philosophy of the district, I was less certain I would be able to implement it. What "counted," if answering correctly, spelling correctly, doing the homework, and passing quizzes and tests did not?

To make a long story short, after spending some time consciously thinking about how, how, how, and what, what, what, I *did* arrive at a solution, although it didn't come easily. Most of my clues came from watching the kids themselves, especially those I had concerns about. *When* did they shine? *What* do they achieve on a daily basis?

I already knew the students loved to participate; all students, regardless of ability, were eager to try out the new sounds. I began to realize some students were creative and divergent in their thinking; others were studious and rigorously correct in all they did. By observing and listening and thinking, I realized I could still count academics as a major part of the class; the "to do" list wasn't going to change or my emphasis on it. What did change, however, was the portion of the grade accounted for by strictly defined academic work (paper and pencil quizzes, homework, tests, writings, responses to readings, etc.). Instead of being approximately 80% of a student's grade, I reduced these items to 33 1/3 percent, which at first seemed a huge "diminishment" of emphasis. But if that was going to be the case, I then had to reexamine my attitude toward participation, from something everyone *had* to do, and therefore was hardly worth attending to, to the notion that participation was something everyone *could* and *did* do and therefore was very much worth attending to, at least 33 1/3 percent!

Finally, it struck me, after one of my most able students created her map of Germany by enlarging the one in the encyclopedia and transferring it to a poster board, that this response to the assignment, although accurate, was not an original one. At the same time, one of my least able students "academically" had free-handed his map of Germany onto the yellow peasant scarf he had sewn in home economics. He included the names, in German, of the neighboring countries as well, most of which were just about legible! (I am not sure even I could have spelled Tschechoslowakei with a felt tipped pen!) His map earned an A. Originality, initiative, and creativity became the final 33 1/3 percent of my grading concept.

"By Jove, I think she's got it!" What I had discovered through this intense period of observing, thinking, and rethinking, is that although my *words* professed love for and interest in German, my *attitude* toward those who were studying it was quite narrow and snobbish. Once I figured out how to maintain regard for the language while simultaneously giving additional attention to the variety of ways kids chose to express *their* care and interest in it, I felt enabled to make the learning and loving of German – or any subject, perhaps – possible for each student, not just the ones who were going to be able to grasp it anyway. My *attitude* toward grading became one of seeking creative opportunities to work with the strengths and challenges of all students. The classroom became a place of possibility for all students, the non-readers, the non-writers, the average kids, and the three gifted students always wanting more. My attitude toward the subject I loved never changed, while my *assumptions* about and *attitude* toward learners had been transformed. Although there is nothing new about my learning as I describe it at the end of the 20th century, it was "new" in a classroom in the 1970s, at least, for me!

I have one last thought. Once I figured out how every student in my classroom could be successful by passing at least two of the three grading components, I was free to imagine a wide variety of types of lessons and successes. I was liberated from the notions that grades are the only measure of success, and success is only measured by written work or oral parallels of it. With such liberation came the ability to create environments connected to the daily work undertaken; it was ever so "academic"! As I stood outside my classroom opening (no door) to greet the students when they entered the long, narrow, windowless classroom (truly an afterthought for the closet when they needed yet another classroom space), they would always ask the same question accompanied by large, curious smiles: "What are we going to do today, Frau Koonts?" (Was machen wir heute?)

And every day, in what became a ritual of pleasant expectation and response, I would reply as eagerly: "Work!" (Arbeit!) I suspect, however, if they remember anything, it has less to do with "der, die, das" than it does with the words to the Oscar Meyer Weiner song! "Meine Wurst hat eine erste Name, sie ist Oh esS Cay Ah aiR...."

As my mom always said, "The only thing you can change about yourself is your attitude." I was challenged by the work of learning, but I had to do it in order to support the learning of my students. But it was they who helped me know what I was supposed to do; their actions, their interests, their responses were the clues I used to detect and discover a different attitude toward them. I will never forget them… Chris, Steve, Beth, Audrey, Ellen, Scott, Mike …

2020

A Awake!

As I reflect on my lengthy engagement with learning and thinking, I am struck by how 'young' I was – and must have sounded – to my principal and colleagues. Although I did a lot of my learning in my head, thinking about things and coming to conclusions and making decisions about future efforts based on those results, I suspect the only thing showing (or was heard in the hallway outside our door) was the enthusiasm we all had for "Arbeit." From my work with freshmen college students, who entered my classroom with an average age of 17, I observed that a demonstrated interest in/enthusiasm for teaching was not the same as enthusiasm for *learning*. The fact I didn't give up on those middle school kids years ago, leaving the principal's office with an "ain't going to work, it's still my way or the highway" attitude, meant I was willing to figure things out. I was willing (and I assume the principal thought I was able) to put in the mental work, the thinking time, to do the job asked of me.

You have to know, at first, I thought the principal was crazy. And then I thought I was *going* crazy. But learning isn't easy. It asks one to change, expand, and grow. As a new teacher, I thought *I* would be the one to foster those verbs in others. Clearly, I had much more to learn beyond my own desire to teach and share what I had learned. As a new college professor, I began to realize working with undergraduate and graduate students was going to give me this opportunity, once again. . . and it certainly did!

Often, the college freshmen with whom I worked thought they knew what it took to be a "good" teacher. One day early in a fall semester, I asked them to tell me. I wrote their responses on the board, filling it. Looking over the concepts, I asked these aspiring teachers, "Which of these qualities are you here to learn about?" There was silence. I rephrased the question: "Okay, why are you in a teacher education program, if not to learn about these qualities?" A young man responded, somewhat tentatively, because no one else was volunteering: "Because we need to take courses in order to get the license so we can teach!" Everyone laughed, nodding in agreement. I followed up with something like, "Given what is on the board, how important are courses about teaching going to be to you, then?" The conclusion the class reached, somewhat embarrassingly expressed, was "not terribly."

There is more to this story, which I may get to later. For now, I am merely concluding that wanting to become a teacher and taking courses to become one is not enough. Were I 17 again, were I thinking about becoming a teacher, I would hope someone would ask me if I would be awake to learning through and beyond what I *expected* to be learning. We have all lived through so many teachers, styles, and expectations; we know "schooling." Were I guiding my own child toward the profession, I think I would become a cheerleader for *learning,* not teaching. **'Awake'**! Be open/ **alert** to what is going on beyond what you assume you are seeing and "learning about." **Ask** questions! **Actualize** the freedom and possibility of your own mind related to the material in any subject/topic you pursue. And pursue many. To beginning teachers, I would most likely say: be the *first* learner in your classroom, among learners. Teach by learning; your students will join you.

1994

B Believe

For many reasons, I choose the verb "to believe" rather than the noun, belief, as my 'b' word. Regardless of the word, however, I am convinced it is in our actions, rather than our talk, that who we are and what we think, feel, and believe is carried out. Whether we choose to believe in a god, an idea, or another person, I think it is the nature of the act of "believing" that makes the impossible possible and the hoped-for real. I know what I believe in is nothing that either makes me special or separates me from millions of other people in this country; with many others I state unequivocally: I believe in children. Believing informs action.

Before "children" is interpreted as an age group, however, let me rephrase. I believe in the child in people. I think it is the child within us who is the learner; she is the risk taker, he is the curious person. Children express wonder, ask direct questions, recognize sincerity; they know when they are confused or "don't get it." Children make sense of things and want to share that sense. Most often, they have room to make a bigger sense of things; they have room to learn more.

Children are also sensitive; they want to be loved and hugged. They want to be acknowledged for the good they do, for their effort, for their original works. Children laugh. Children imagine learning as an adventure in which I am also a participant, not merely or somehow more importantly, "the teacher." These qualities of the child are qualities I seek in the learners with whom I work, whether they are colleagues, graduate students, or freshmen in college. They are the qualities I seek in my friends.

I believe in sharing my enthusiasm for learning with others. I believe the best teachers are confident learners; they are people in action. They are inquisitive; they seek additional resources and the newest information or different combinations of the old; they also maximize resources and find ways to work with others through *their* ideas to support learning.

I also believe in hard work, in the spirit of living some would call Christmas, in the earth as a source of life and inspiration. I believe I am loved and am therefore best able to share my love with others. Most of all, I believe it is important to believe; to have faith in others, in spite of their humanity, which I clearly share. I believe my life is a gift I need to honor as the lives of my students are a treasure to treat with kindness and respect. I teach to honor *their* possibility; I keep learning and, therefore, I believe, I honor my own.

An old Mary Engelbreit holiday tin depicts a Santa Claus laden with a bag of toys; the single word upon the bottom border is "BELIEVE." This tin is displayed in my living room all year round as is this "action" in my work with others. I believe in that unfilled space, in coloring "beyond the lines." To believe is to have purpose; to have purpose is to act. As a learner, how could I not teach? My actions = my believes.

2020

B Believe?

The other day I heard on the radio that some are calling this last year in the 2nd decade of the 21st century the "age of anxiety." It would be naïve to say my thoughts on "believe" and "belief" haven't changed. Yet, I struggle to grasp all the believes out there, some of which challenge the core of my hopefulness. Within the past year I saw a news broadcast about the suicide of a 17-year-old girl, a star in every sense from a clearly engaged and loving family; I was heartbroken, again. Excerpts from her journal read "I AM A FAILURE" or "I am WORTHLESS." Evidence in the real world, among all who knew her, was to the contrary. No doubt my believing in children, the students with whom I worked, *was probably never enough* and was, perhaps, even annoying, because I *didn't* know what was going on with them. I really didn't 'learn' them very well at all.

Where to start then? What is the 'b' word for the 21st century, and what can teachers do to support their students' finding it, using it, and valuing it? Thoughts are skittering across my mind like the dry, brown leaves lightly tumbling across the expanse of frozen snow in my yard. I am thinking about Montessori; I am thinking of the woman who wrote *Teacher* (1963); I am thinking of poets and artists and athletes. I am remembering the research about children of divorce and the term "resilience," which seems similar to this century's idea of "grit."

At a time when there is so much emphasis on social media, I don't think I am talking about being a cheerleader or a cock-eyed optimist. I *am* thinking of asking each child, in his or her own time with me, 'Who are you? What do you like to do?' Maybe I would have liked to have met these 24 young people before we ever met in the classroom, because the distance on day one, "Hello, I'm X and what's your name?" is such a formal way to begin learning together and among others. It *is* a wall, a boundary, isn't it? In a century where technology simultaneously brings us together and separates us ever more, walls between human beings are not what we need.

When students return to schools, in whatever the post-COVID19 iteration may be, news reports tell us the children "will be 'behind.'" What does "being behind" have to do with *children*, who haven't seen their grandparents, who aren't playing with their friends, and who are as old as they have ever been? How can they be behind? Behind what?

Is there a time and place where we can get to know them, again, to support their learning from where they are *today*? They will not be the same children/students who left you, nor will you be the same teachers. Please don't put the burden of 'being behind' on yourself or them; there *is* no "behind"! Learning is *always* today's opportunity: where do we find ourselves today, what can we accomplish today, what might that mean for tomorrow? Let's find out! On your mark, get set, let's learn!

In conclusion then, what would my 'b' word be today? Buoyancy? Boundary? Perhaps biography. I would encourage any teacher or anyone thinking about teaching to read the first few chapters of *Teacher* (Ashton-Warner, 1963) in order to appreciate the "problem" of having students she could not communicate with, in her language or theirs. How *do* we, as teachers, cultivate learning as a life-long infection rather than a deadly disease? Maybe it starts in understanding the biography of the individuals with whom we work a bit more intimately – not the notes passed up from the last teacher, but from one-on-one time with the student? Maybe a home visit? Teachers used to do that, didn't they? I know there are some who still do, because it is their learning and the *connection* between the two that strengthens student learning and fosters the possible. But that's a 'c' word, isn't it?

Biography, then – not on paper, but through the eyes, gestures, and stories of ones, however young. Through it are the bridges to stronger learning and knowing. It is not a verb, yet it is, with every breath we take.

1994

| C | **Curiosity** (among other concepts)

One of the biggest **challenge**s can be catching students' attention, leading them – especially as they get older – to become curious about things they have either begun to take for granted or toward which they assume they have no interest. I teach a course in assessment to upper class preservice teachers at 8:00 in the morning. The biggest **commitment** many of them make is simply showing up; expecting them to inquire about "authentic assessment" and "standardized tests" may be presuming too much. Although I don't remember being an annoying two-year old asking "WHY?" after every statement, I suspect I have become a rather annoying adult, asking my students, colleagues, and friends, "Why is that?" "Why do you think they took that point of view?" "What does it mean if we assume this is the case?" "Why might I disagree with this critique?" etc., etc., etc.!

Perhaps I am **curious** beyond the norm; perhaps because I am interested in how we make sense of things, questions of why come naturally to me. I want to know what is going on; I am interested in motivations and lack of them; I am interested in purposes and the results of thinking and doing. Mostly, I am curious about what the people with whom I interact think and feel about things. I have an "inquiring mind." I *want* to know!

When I was 17 and a senior in high school, a young man who was the son of friends of my parents suggested that when I replied "I don't know" to some of his questions, I was really saying, "I don't want to *think* about that right now, and even if I *did* think about it, I am not sure about where my thoughts would take me, and so rather than answer your questions, I'll simply say, 'I don't know.' It's easier!" He accused me of "copping out," an expression of the times.

Two years older than I and already in college, David was most certainly the smartest guy I had ever met. He scared me a little, but he also challenged me to express my thoughts and to be curious about those of others. He was not satisfied with a superficial analysis of anything (yes, he *was* a bit intense!). He challenged me *to think about what I thought*. I also found it curious, and somewhat exciting, that he wanted to know, but there's a different story!

During the last twenty years, I have tried to engage my students' minds in a similar, less intimidating way. Whether they are 6th graders listening to German sounds for the first time or doctoral students explaining their thesis ideas to me at a conference, I am curious about what these learners are thinking and how the ideas they are working with come together for them. My curiosity, then, goes beyond general inquisitiveness; in the classroom, I try to model thinking beyond the simple comprehension of facts and their relationships. I find I am a committed learner; if by modeling questions rather than answers and curiosity rather than certainty I enable some students to become more willing to try out an answer that may not be in the book (and therefore, somehow, "incorrect"), then these students will begin to get a sense that in our community of learners questions are a *good* thing; they will begin to believe *not knowing* as a way of discovering is okay; they will gain confidence in expressing possibilities and following leads rather than feeding back the author's words, which I am almost certain are never incorporated into their permanent understandings anyway. It is the students' understandings that are carried away with them. Without curiosity, the learning is not for them – it is for the grade, the teacher, the parents. With it, mine and theirs, theirs and mine, learning becomes the adventure of our lives together.

C Caring

As I reread, I have two thoughts. First, I suspect most teachers already *do* the things I was imagining 25 years ago. Second, I realize how many other thoughts and 'c' words come to mind. I think of what I learned about **compassion** from dear **colleagues,** who also became most special friends, Dr. Radha Bhatkal and Dr. Joan Mulligan. Another colleague taught me about the power of "YES," Dr. John Duval, which will come later. But were I in a 21st century classroom, I think I would like to learn much more about paths to **conflict resolution**. Having a greater understanding of how to resolve differences, whether with students, colleagues, or parents, would bolster my capacity to reassure all with whom I work that I hear what I listen to and have some wisdom, some strategies, to deescalate competing "wants." Until this moment, I had not really thought about the supplemental/the **complementary curriculum** that would support teachers both novice and expert in their daily efforts. Our student teachers used to tell us what they needed or wished they had learned. I think I need to head back to my 'a' word and assert that *asking* for what you need – and then seeking and finding it – will only foster **confidence** in how you interact with others. Confidence, it seems to me, provides more room for compassion. Compassion is grounded in **caring**, a concept Nel Noddings, a high school math teacher become philosophy professor at Stanford University during the last two decades of the 20th century, believed was important enough to explicate and legitimize within the educational research community and beyond. (see References, p. 83) I think this last 'c' word, then, grounds not only the other 'c' concepts, but also, undoubtedly, the entire alphabet itself. Hmm.

1994

D Delight

It is 1994. Sometimes, I think I have been in this profession for too long, because it is at times like these I consider trying something *really* new, like learning how to drive an 18-wheeler! I think, 'maybe I'm just not good at meetings,' or 'maybe this class just isn't getting it,' or 'maybe I haven't focused clearly enough,' or 'maybe they aren't doing their homework.' In writing these thoughts, the teeter-totter of me-them seems out of balance; one end is inevitably heavier than the other when these gaps or off-putting moments capture my attention.

In my most serious moments, I blame myself. For example, am I pre-occupied with this other event or issue in my life? Is my difficult morning at home translating into a difficult morning with my students? On the other hand, in moments just as serious, I blame my students: Why do they think the minimum effort is worth the maximum grade? Does effort equal achievement? Is it enough to simply *be* in the room?

Experience has shown me, however, that when I am in a sad or preoccupied state, my students seem to sense this and come to my rescue in some way. I will never forget the absolutely huge card my "after lunch" 6th grade German class made for me one year. They had asked the social studies teacher to distract me at the end of study hall so they would have time to get to class first. When I walked in (we are back in the room described in letter 'a' that looks and feels like a long, windowless closet), all of the lights were off. When I went back into the hallway to switch them on and then reenter the class, the 6th graders yelled "SURPRISE!!!" and looked at me with such anticipation. The huge card read, "This is NOT a birthday card, this is NOT a Merry

Christmas card, this card is simply to say…WE LOVE YOU FRAU KOONTS!!" I was so touched I had to walk out of the room to catch my breath. My marriage was in serious difficulty; although I thought I didn't bring it into the day-to-day classroom, the kids clearly felt I needed a little love. I was overwhelmed; *of course* I cried! They thought my reaction meant I was mad at them. How is that possible?! I explained tears of joy, and they relaxed back into their exuberant, after-lunch selves.

Students sometimes read *us* better than any other text they are presented with. They know if we like what we are doing, they know if we like them. They know if we are disappointed or tired. They also know if we take delight in being there with them, in teaching and in learning, in knowing a little bit about them, and in wondering out loud about what we don't know. I know I take delight in the small gains of challenged students; in a moment of creativity from a conforming, gifted student; in student projects from other classes, or someone's new glasses, outfit, or haircut.

I know I am not alone in this level of attention. For many, there has been that every once-in-a-horrific-while when we are reminded of the *vulnerability* of human beings, reminding us to take ever more delight in the lives that are ours and theirs in this moment. We all die a little when a child dies. Each day, each *they*, is precious.

What I have shown my students of delight, I do not really know. But the notion of being able to offer moments of non-judgmental pleasure toward each of them as individuals and as a class as a whole seems close to delight. Perhaps because students are "supposed" to be the learners, I assume I get much more from them as they discover, think, apply, and evaluate their work. In recognition of my own standards of care and thought put toward achievement, however, I am uncertain what, if any, delight they take away! I know they remember my enthusiasm for teaching and learning, which may or may not be the same thing, and of course, it is not all I *want* them to remember.

I do know in my own professional life that when I receive a well-written critique of proposals or articles – the exception, not the rule by the way – I am deeply appreciative of the effort and care someone took with me and my words. Although "delighted" is not *exactly* what I'm feeling, I am able to continue to reflect, respond, and grow as a result of that interest. No one "delights" in criticism, but I am so grateful when someone takes the time and care to do it *well*. It makes me think the time and effort put in so far was worth it. I am trying to use this learning as I work with graduate students in research, although receiving good criticism is much easier than generating it. Self-editing is a skill that takes practice.

Anyway, just because we get older does not mean we are less susceptible to someone else's sincere pleasure in our existence. Delight = from the light. Exuberance. Joy. Enthusiasm. The result of noticing. An attitude toward learning; an expression of loving. And sometimes, the point of a bad attempt at humor: "Justin, please will you turn up de-light?"

2019

| D | Delight! |

As I type, reflecting on 'd' words, I don't think there is a better one than delight. I offer this word only because I don't know after how many words, years, and students later, I keep remembering faces of 'ah hah' and satisfaction, as well as some genuine pride in the power of one's individual good work. As I reread what I wrote, I suddenly think of shy Jessica, the only sophomore in a Foundations of Education class in 2008 made up of several juniors and transfer students. She was "young" in her educational career, having just decided to become a teacher; she loved her family and horses. Her colleagues were older, more proficient learners. Her experience with difficult material and verbal colleagues was one of incremental, increased learning and understanding; by the close of the semester, her maturity, comprehension, and capacity shone like the ease of her ready smile.

I saw her just recently, in TJ Maxx. There she was, experienced teacher, married woman, home owner. And I know one thing. She will read these letters, these thoughts between me and you, and tell me if I have it right. She will tell me where I need to express myself more clearly; she will tell me what touches her, what works for her. To have her face and essence appear before me as I was reading about delight tells you how powerful such a word is, how powerful taking delight in the learning is. Like the strengthening light of day into the mid-morning hours, we often take it for granted. That I still know her, that she is her own powerful woman and teacher, brings delight. I am keeping this word! It *is* an action, grown from the inside out and from the unknown to the possible. YES!

1994

E Energy

Whether you eat Wheaties, work-out, run, sing, dance, cook, read, yodel, travel, garden, or fish, without energy we simply live our lives less well. In schools, we have energy-draining days, activities, and colleagues; we also have energy-enhancing days, activities, and colleagues. Sunlight gives us energy, as do "mental health" days. Chocolate works, for a while. Perhaps even more energizing is a group of people working together on a new idea, where each supports the strengths others bring to it, where agreement is reached to move forward with something derived from the discussion, and the burden of effort is shared (see letter 'h'). Energy begets energy. People working with each other, trying something new, together, can be life-enhancing.

Sometimes, my classroom has been like that. And sometimes, there is nothing worse than facing a group of students who sit there like bumps on a log. If I am able to maneuver to the back of the classroom, or behind the circle, then I don't have to look at them. I can then imagine interested faces; I ask a question, allow appropriate wait/think time, and then call on the back of a student. We may get started slowly, but I begin with a question they can all answer. Energy is not about throwing a switch and expecting the light; more often than not, it is about finding the sticks to rub together, sending some kids out for more kindling while having several others attend to the nascent idea, to act as bellows to the spark.

Energy. Remember those middle schoolers I mentioned earlier? I remember allowing a silent, below-the-face, paper wad fight (of course there were rules!), or sending them outside to run around the building three times without making a sound (except "pant, pant"). Energy. "Repeat after me!" (Wiederholen Sie, Bitte!) "Let's look it up!" "What did you bring in today?" "What did you think about the assignment?" "What was your reaction to the big story on the news last night?" "How does this topic pertain to your lives today?" "What affect will this information have on your decision making?" Energy, to ask questions requiring thought. Thought requires energy. Energy begets energy. Together, learner and learners, we have synergy.

Some kids don't eat right. Some kids don't sleep comfortably or safely. Some kids spend all of their energy on survival. Maybe if we could create enough energy in our own classrooms, we would have enough left over to make a difference in our communities, in lasting ways; we could change things. We could work, as I am sure many of you do, to get students to apply what they learn in active ways outside the classroom. To use learning requires energy. Energy needs a source. Maybe that is de-light. And attitude. And believe. And homes in a community that cares, a synonym for loving?

2020

| E | **Economize!**

As I reread my thoughts on energy, I remember clearly noticing it – and the lack thereof – while teaching, perhaps because I value it in learners. I have had several teachers in my past who exhibited no energy whatsoever. In a high school history class, we very unkindly placed bets on how long it would take our teacher's drool to drop onto his notes on the desk. It was awful. Yet, the class counted toward our grade point average; we were stuck. Clearly events of the past were more interesting than our teacher's lack of energy in the present, but we never found that out, nor were we inspired to do so. (hmm…students seem to expect a lot from teachers, don't they?)

I have two examples that helped me learn and appreciate the role of energy. Even if it is "good," even if it is "enthusiastic," energy can be a detriment to students' learning when it gets in their faces, becomes more of a focus than the topic, or when it doesn't allow room for *student* interests and discoveries to be made, exclaimed, and shared.

Did I ever really "know" what I am saying now? I don't think so. If you hadn't guessed, I'm a rather intense, energized kind of teacher, talking while walking, using my hands. Having energy towards work was a value taught in my family. I can't say I always loved raking the yard, for example, but I cannot do it now without hearing my father's voice: "You missed a leaf!" All I had accomplished, all the effort and subsequent satisfaction upon seeing the still green grass free of fall's crazy quilt, dissipated. What had I accomplished, after all? What effort would gain approval?

It wasn't until early in my college teaching career, when I was watching two graduate students give a presentation to their peers, that I began to question the whole concept of teacher energy/enthusiasm/ excitement. The two young women were enthralled with their topic (I think it was "whole language"); they moved around in front of us, used the board, provided hand outs and visuals. They were almost breathless with their preparations; their enthusiasm, I assumed, would be infectious. They could hardly wait for us to grab onto their understandings and jump on the bandwagon.

That is not what happened. From my perspective behind all of the students, it seemed the more energy the speakers produced, the more excited they were to share, the less energy and interest their peers seemed to have, if their body language was any indication. No one was holding a pen, and shoulders were slumped. By the end of the presentation, most were using one arm to hold their heads up; I saw no one lean forward with rapt attention. "How'd we do?!," the presenters asked when it was over.

Before analyzing this example for alternative, possible explanations, let me give the second example, which sharpened the "it is just a feeling I did nothing with" to something concrete I could grasp. It was only many years later, probably during my last semester or two of observing student teachers, when I noticed one second grade teacher in particular. Although I observed mostly in middle and secondary schools, every so often I was asked to supervise a student or two seeking elementary licensure. By this point in time, I felt confident in what I was seeing in the aspiring teachers, because I had worked with many competent to outstanding elementary mentors in our region. This semester would be my second time as a participant observer in Jean Pritchard's second grade classroom. I knew our student was in good hands. During early observations, I "suddenly" understood everything I had not quite been able to put into words: Energy, Enthusiasm, and Excitement have their place in a classroom, but neither is it the *first* place, nor is it the teacher's *first* job to exhibit it. Having it is important; Jean does. Restraining it, remaining consistent but not overwhelming with it gives student learners room to find their own places of excitement, curiosity, and knowledge, especially young learners. I saw it happen. Another of her more exuberant colleagues, Mark Rampone, creates a similar space, but differently. Both share tremendous, yet bounded, joy.

Among such educators, I finally understood what incredible patience and self-restraint being a leader of young/early learning requires. It occurred to me that perhaps I *could* become an elementary teacher with appropriate learning and professional development, even if I will still never be able to fit into those tiny chairs! And so, it also occurred to me that the graduate student "audience" so long ago might have already *learned* about the topic, therefore exhibiting less interest in it? Their colleague "teachers" never asked what they knew and how much they knew about the topic, almost the first questions elementary mentors modeling best practice ask when a new subject is broached.

A teacher's demeanor is one of the first things beyond appearance that students notice. As high schoolers, we noticed the drool and never made it to history. The graduate students sat politely listening to their peers but may never have embraced whole language. Almost like punishment, a teacher's passion can become a tsunami just as the lack thereof can become a shroud. Hence, the 'e' word after more thought is "economize." Perhaps it would be better to suggest that self-control, while sharing delight, helps to create a learning environment where student learning takes center stage. We go to a symphony and listen to the orchestra. If the conductor is doing it right, if they have all done the requisite work, then that role, the conductor's work, goes almost unnoticed.

One of my favorite educational researchers, arts educator Elliot Eisner, once said something like the following to a ballroom full of educational researchers, professors, and administrators: 'If we do our jobs ever better, we won't have our jobs in the future.' As I stood to applaud him, I was yanked back down in my seat by others at my table (I was sitting way up front, adoration in my eyes, and so on). Of *course* no one in the room applauded! We were there meeting *because* of our jobs; we *need* our work. Our work is to keep *control* of learning so that students and schools will *need* us, provide *us* with jobs?! Really? I'll stop. I'll economize. The point is simply that we ought not be the center of student learning; our work and energy need to create ever larger opportunities for theirs.

1994

F Fun = Work = Learning

Imagine these three concepts as corners of a triangle, softened by believe, opportunity, curiosity, and delight.

2020

The Challenge of Learning makes the Work Fun for me!

I have changed the heading but not the equation itself. I wrote it; it makes sense to me. I remember hating the old discussions about "learning isn't fun, it's work" or "learning should be fun, in order for kids to learn." There are research studies discussing both opinions. We do know students learn more and better if they are engaged with each other and with the subject. What makes a subject engaging is often the "fly" teachers have to attach to the "hook" the subject at hand is. I was reading a book about fishing, seriously, I was, and different fish, in different streams at different times, take different bait. A serious fisherperson has more than one fly. No doubt most of you reading this have used many to get things started. To change metaphors, maybe you had to provide the kindling – or maybe a student idea became the focus – and even more likely, regardless of curriculum, once lit you had to blow on it a little, preview it with a real world example or a question about their knowledge. You *know* this one. Teachers like using their minds and hearts to make amazing things possible. That is synergy of another kind. And it is work. But it is what learning inspires, and as such, the work is fun. Let's roast some marshmallows on that fire!

1994

G Grace

This 'g' word is special to me for a variety of reasons. First, my students are ever witness to the lack thereof as I move around the classroom, bumping into their desks or the corner of mine, tripping over the overhead projector cord, not seeing the wall behind me, or simply missing the door! The "full" part of graceful I am, but not, unfortunately, the grace part.

Second, grace seems a quality a klutz can aspire to; however, I am sure *only if I stand still* might I attain it! Third, my youngest niece's middle name is Grace. Hi, Lydia Grace!

Yourdictionary.com offers the following definitions of grace: (*italics are mine*)

1. beauty or charm of form, composition, movement, or expression; elegance with appropriate dignity; as, she danced with much grace
2. an attractive quality, feature, manner, etc.

In its third meaning, grace is appropriate for teachers and learners:
3. *a sense of what is right and proper; decency*

In its fourth meaning, grace can mean our goodwill toward ourselves and others; in teaching and learning, grace is often depended upon:

4. *[a] disposition to grant something freely;* favor; *good will;*

Grace has several additional meanings:

5. *mercy;* clemency

6. a period of time granted beyond the date set for the performance of an act or the payment of an obligation; temporary exemption

How we approach a late paper or a computer break-down might just require a little grace; some assignments for some students might need the infamous "grace period!"

Finally, in my home, we always said *grace* before dinner. As I think of things to be thankful for, beyond my students and my life, I do believe in the love of a god upon us all.

7. ...in theology, the free unmerited love and favor of God...

2020

| G | Grace |

Well, it's not the first time I have said it, but I am sticking by this one, as a verb this time. Having grace, modeling grace in physical interaction, interpersonal communication, and as a 'quality of being' related to one's treatment of one's self and others, is something only we can hold ourselves accountable for. We do so, I think, because about some things in this world, we teachers are simply right. *How* we communicate our rightness may make all the difference in how *well* we are heard.

1994

H Harmony

In music, harmony infers more than one voice, yet it is not consensus, as different voices have separate and unlike lines. It is true in literature, we and the protagonist learn much from conflict, when things *aren't* harmonious. In life, from each other's opinions and knowledge, we discover areas of agreement or continued difference.

Harmony implies difference in the patterns of notes played at the same time, difference which highlights, deepens, softens, or echoes a theme.

Harmony illuminates varied strengths while holding them together in a pattern that recognizes the interdependence of single voices' greater power in combination.

Harmony requires knowledge of and about the instruments and their capacities, the students and their strengths and challenges.

Harmony requires planning, attention to particulars without losing a sense of the whole. Harmony enables even as it may divide attention.

Harmony is working together, each with a part. It is easy enough to be the lead voice and have the others learn the more difficult ones. Teachers already know about whales and whole numbers; they know how to read. Teaching is often a solo act, sometimes acapella. As nice as all that may be, harmony is a richer act; it requires more of and from the teacher who fosters students' abilities to lead, hit the high notes, set the beat, or change the key, or even, perhaps, the score itself. To be still requires a teacher, who, as a learner, is able to harmonize or perhaps merely hum in the background. Teachers, indeed, need to "know the score," but they must also nurture, guide, and protect a child's voice, even when correction may be the task.

2012

H Hypothesize

If I did not include some kind of research word in this book, I would be dissing my own educational background. At the same time, this term isn't here because of my background. I think this action – a formal one in scientific settings – was more recently brought home to me by a kindergarten student, who, upon arriving early to his classroom, went right over to the guinea pig corral at the side of the room to observe the furry creature currently munching on something. The teacher noticed both of our arrivals to the classroom and, after a quick welcome, went over near the student, took a seat at his level and asked how he was? Fine. Do you want to feed Harold (or whatever the name was)? Yes.

The boy took some of the lettuce from its container nearby. As he put it into the corral, he asked his teacher, "Why doesn't he eat that?" pointing to the cedar shavings abundant on the floor.

So far, nothing unexpected. So far, I might have predicted both individuals' behaviors, but I had not predicted what happened next. I agree I *should* have for, as I have mentioned before, I worked with many wonderful mentor teachers.

"Why do *you* think he doesn't eat that?" she asked him.

What followed was a fascinating experience watching a very small person – I was in a K-2 setting – try to figure out what to say to the teacher. The short version (I still have my notes somewhere about this moment) says he looked up and away and around and down, kind of shrugged his shoulders and said, "I think it has something to do with the wind." How so? "Well, it's light and could blow away and you can't eat air." Okay. Why do you think he eats the lettuce? "Because it is green like the ground, and they eat green." By this time, other students were entering the classroom. The teacher concluded the interaction by saying, "We will talk about this again. Save your question to ask your classmates; we will discuss it further."

How many times – whether to friends, colleagues, students – did I give an answer rather than ask a question about their question? Isn't an answer what is asked for? Isn't it easier to give? In 2008, when searching for some new way to organize my first and only Foundations of Education class *not* comprised of incoming freshmen, I came upon Deanna Kuhn's book, *Education as Thinking*. In it, she gives an example similar to what I had just experienced, although the researcher pressed the student more directly and did not let up immediately. When my foundations students read the example, their adjectives describing the teacher/researcher were "cold," "intimidating," "unhelpful," "mean." The question they had for me was: Why didn't she just *answer* him?

That question – and the answer – is at the crux of learning, its essence, I think. My knowing something doesn't by necessity mean you will *learn* it upon hearing my answer. In fact, it probably means you won't have to explore the notion any further? I may have satisfied an immediate curiosity and felt edified by doing so, but I have done nothing to nurture and further the learning and subsequent knowing → understanding of the questioner, have I? Maybe that is a hypothesis I should further test. What do you think?

2020

"at its best, schooling can be about how to make a life, which is quite different from how to make a living"(x).

It is the cusp of Summer 2020. In the self-isolation/social distancing days when I do see my neighbor and his two grown children, and when I do get the opportunity to listen to what they are thinking about, I am reminded – following their father's example – there *are* things I haven't thought of, perspectives I might not have anticipated.

Listening, asking for more information and/or clarification is ... informing. I am reminded of being a learner once again. It is such a pleasure!

It would be one thing if the issue were one of "just the facts," but the entire country is debating even those. The structure of schools – from the day through the curriculum – remains largely focused on a program that tests knowledge acquisition to a greater degree than it fosters applications in the "real" world. Having exploratory sessions around alternative hypotheses related to history, literature, art, science, current events, always felt like a luxury, a time out from "the regular classroom." As we reimagine what for many of us is yet another attempt to envision a better, fair, and just world for our students, I think we are going to have to come up with new answers and unimagined possibilities that shake up not only the bottle corporate maple syrup comes in but also the fundamentals of curriculum and "schooling" we have taken for granted for so long, even when and if we *know* and work in *individual* ways to make learning more expansive and the school day "better" than a series of subjects to get through. Bringing public education into the middle of the 21st century and beyond will require taking the dinosaur by the tail, even if it is the comfortable herbivore keeping the grass cut low. Perhaps only a giant asteroid can wipe it out; more likely, we need a giant amount of shared will. Check out letter 'y'! Who says we can't change? Neil Postman's (1995) *The End of Education* argues thoughtfully for an alternative curricular imagination and offers suggestions that can be both easily grasped and acted upon. The quotation with which I began this section comes from the preface of Postman's book.

How could we/do we move forward from here? There is an opportunity *not* to return to the same things that tend to frustrate or disappoint, but in order for such to happen, there are things we have to know: What happened as you taught this spring 2020? What new essentials emerged, and what other things, long a part of your day, disappeared ...maybe even happily so? What are you learning?

1996

⬛ I Intellect

The kids of the 21st century face a more complex environment than ever before. Much will depend upon their abilities to access, evaluate, and use information. It is not enough for them to go to school and simply "slurp and burp." Comparing alternatives, weighing choices, and determining value, for example, are skills that are not historical facts, literary themes, or mathematical equations. They are, however, qualities that can be honed through the study of facts, themes, and equations. More than ever before our students need to foster their ability to look at the world from a variety of perspectives. We will need their insights sooner than we ever have before. We need their minds and hearts and hopes. We need *their* intellect, not our "right" answers. We need their *capabilities*, not their test scores. We need their interest in learning; we can gain that by learning their interests; communication is not unilateral. The top-down, bureaucratic, factory model of schools is so long out of date and out of touch. Communities of learners, where learning is celebrated, is the buzz term at the turn of the century. We should not be afraid of intellect or developing the communities within which it is nurtured; it is a quality of mind we need to notice and hone.

I am still working this letter out. As much as I encourage my juniors and seniors to think for themselves, and I tell them I will honor their thoughts, I find some believe what I mean is that *whatever* they think is okay. If this is true, so the logic seems to be, then they don't have to read the text I have chosen for them, nor do they have to find additional source material or incorporate what we learned yesterday into their answers for today. I am clearly not "there" in terms of working with them in ways that force them to challenge what is in their minds or challenge what is in the text by finding corroborating or contradictory resources.

It is a scary thing being a preservice teacher upon the eve of student teaching; if one doesn't feel prepared, then I find there is a "circle the wagons" tendency, to at least be confident about what one *does* know. Trouble is, these kids/new teachers have only just begun. If they are already "certain" about some things (usually their past experiential learning in schools), then the ordinary classroom and textbook knowledge will not add to their "known" very much, except with the acquisition of basic, additional "facts." Enabled opinions, better thought processes, openness to ideas without fear of being "graded" are not the current results of time-test educational practice. No matter how much more we know about teaching and learning, no students want to give the "wrong" answer or do merely "satisfactory" work. Honing the intellect, like stropping the blade, takes patience and skill.

The intellect has been left out of our achievement goals; it is a quality of mind both "born" and "made." Fostering children's innate curiosity, providing the resources from which they can formulate answers – and even greater questions – is worth the effort. "I think, therefore, I am…" I think!

2020

I HypothesIze!

Seriously, I am not looking for a way out, but as I reread what I wrote above, I sense the link between my current thinking related to the H word. My hunch is to say more here would be redundant? Except, perhaps, I would now take exception to the statement full of assumptions I made above…did you catch it? *"As much as I encourage my juniors and seniors to think for themselves…."* WOW! Did I never honor my freshmen's thinking in the same way? My middle-schoolers? What did I assume then? Now? If that writing was my thoughtful best, was I still making teacher-led assumptions – after twenty years of teaching – about what my work was and theirs, as well as about their abilities and capacities as learners? Did I even *think* about learning from the perspective of them as *thinkers*?

Kuhn (2005) argues for a curriculum structured on the foundational processes of inquiry and argumentation; through these two processes, learners can discover, locate, and figure out any subject they wish to explore, no longer limited by an adult learner's interests or a curriculum's expectations. I used the Kuhn book in 2008 (see 2020 'd' word), when I was already teaching as an adjunct professor in my own department. I remain convinced Kuhn's argument for such a curriculum is an argument for the strengthening of every learner's ability to go it alone, with confidence and dignity, to thrive in our classrooms and beyond. This description defines the "empowerment" word often discussed in the late 1970s/early 80s, one that hung me up on what felt like "too much teacher" in the definition. Perhaps that is because almost 40 years ago, teachers *were* the focus. I am grateful for the ongoing changes in teaching and learning honoring both educators' and students' possibilities.

1994

[J] Jump (courage)

Actually, 'j' is a segue to another 'c' word, "courage." Courage, as a quality of living and thinking, is rarely on top of a teacher's or learner's value list.

I have observed elementary classrooms and taught every grade level above them. What I have noticed is that many students are still waiting to be taught, especially initially as they encounter a new classroom/grade level, or a new teacher. They are still waiting to be told what to do, discover what is expected of them, and figure out how they can earn the "A." Current research is forecasting that *college* students of the future, having come from more diverse, multi-age, inquiry-based classrooms, will be different. They will not be so willing to sit still for lecture and long, written assignments. These students will demand collaborative learning opportunities; they will expect to have some voice in the direction the course takes, and they will expect valid alternatives to paper and pencil testing.

I eagerly await this future. In the meantime, I work to expose our prospective teachers to a variety of possible areas of interest and inquiry within (and even out from) our explicit purpose for meeting. I also make it clear such opportunities are not classroom expectations. For example, I offer the freshmen samples from my bookshelves or ask them to find a book of interest to read before the end of the semester. I suggest at the end of the term we will share any of the ideas or thoughts they read about. I also describe the opportunity as a "non-assignment"; it does not appear on the syllabus, and it will not be graded.

"What does that mean? What if we don't do it?"

"What do you think?" I reply.

"It won't affect our grade?" they respond, in disbelief.

"No, it won't affect your grade one bit. I am asking you to do it, but I won't demand it. You have talked about the special teachers in your lives; reread your list of characteristics. I can't "make" you be like them. Although there are many "good" teachers out there, it takes something more to be that memorable one. How much effort are you willing to make? How much do you want to know, in order to be "the best?" Can *I* tell you how to be *your* best? Do you know what your best *is*? If so, are you going to be your best "for me" or for your students? Both? When does it count?"

Darn. It would be so much easier if I would tell them: "Do this, it is part of your grade." These students are freshmen, their identities as young adults are taking shape even as I write. They know how to behave and to write reasonably well. Looking at their performance now that we are 8-10 weeks into the semester, wouldn't it just be easier to give them assignments they have to do for grades, expecting the same things from all of them? What does any of this have to do with courage?

Research undertaken in the middle eighties suggested teachers share a set of characteristics: they are of average intelligence, they come from moderate to conservative households, and they are, for the most part, conformists. They are also, for the most part, sincere people. They "mean" well, and they care about children. However, research undertaken in the 50s/early 60s suggested that these characteristics, particularly behaving well and conforming to the norm, are *not* characteristics of *learners*. Learners are not often the best-behaved students; they challenge their teachers and classroom norms. They have shorter attention spans; they seek connections and applications for their learning.

Shortly after reading and thinking about "learners" in graduate school, I returned home for a visit with my middle-school colleagues. I was so excited to ask them if they knew that what we valued and emphasized as "good" learners had little to do with learning! When I shared my insight, a few laughed, and one said: "Why Judy, but of course. If we can't control them, if their behavior isn't "good," then how can we ever teach them?"

I recall mumbling something like "we'll have to teach them as they learn then," but I may have actually said nothing at all. I was so disappointed. I had expected they would be thrilled to hear what I was learning and thinking, or at the very least they would entertain the thought. I share this moment, because the courage *not* to know something and the courage not to be *right* seems rare among us who profess to care about *learning?* At the least, it sure felt like that at the time.

The results of *not* having courage, of *not* being open to change and difference and challenge are all around us. Magazines and TV news shows have been filled up for years with "restructuring schools" and how "some" schools are changing. But what about individual classrooms? How many of us, as teachers, have the courage not to know? to allow apparent "chaos"? to explore territories of interest to kids? And even if we have this courage, how many school leaders would en*courage* us to do so? When it comes time to assess such learning, are we finding ways to honor the adventure of learning while critiquing, in a formative way, achievement and intellectual progress? Isn't it easier to tell our students their ideas are not strong enough, or are simply wrong? Isn't a test easier to score than a portfolio piece? Isn't a short essay easier than an extended one and both easier than determining performance and product criteria, which consider both content and process knowledge? And what is wrong with easy when the ongoing structure, format, and processes of schooling take up so much of a teacher's time and energy? "We have to stop before the bell rings!"; "…only 15 minutes for this activity…"; "Oh, they are into it, but we have to do math now." What does any of this have to do with courage?

In the 21st century, the onslaught of change will confront all of us ever faster. Keeping up with changes in technology and information, as well as the impact of both of these upon the average human being is a challenge most of us acknowledge but are less sure about ways to handle. Teachers in the 21st century cannot wait to be told how to deal with it. They cannot afford to wait until someone in authority says "jump." Teachers in the 21st century need to understand the directions of change, the potential advantages and pitfalls of new science and reconstructed histories. Teachers in the 21st century must be sure of their own voices; they must trust their investigative skills and hone their critical capacities; they must be able not only to work independently but also interdependently. Most assuredly, they must continue to care.

Acting, instead of reacting, requires courage. Becoming a self-motivated learner is a challenge for almost everyone, because it implies two simple truths, which are, "I do not know it all," and "learning is work." Admitting that takes courage. When we consider the old model of a teacher as the knower in a classroom, the challenge in front of us is clear. I am not debasing knowing; I am only acknowledging its space next to that of learning. Simply put, teachers-to-be in the 21st century will have to extend their capacity for learning more than ever before. They will have to acknowledge comfortably and with confidence that they "don't know"; they cannot afford to be threatened by gaps in their own experience or knowledge or by the interests and directions of their students. They cannot expect to consider the role of teacher without valuing the challenge the role of learner requires. We may already value the "learners" in our classrooms; in the 21st century, we will need to value the learner in *ourselves* and give it a place of honor in our teaching. That takes courage.

When I was in college, I remember reading a book, Paul Tillich's, *The Courage to Be*. I went back and found it a few years ago; it is quite dense, which is clearly the reason I only remembered the title! Until now, normative classroom behavior demands the reward of a grade for knowledge acquisition (achievement). Enabling students to learn how to learn, to make connections across learnings and to think for themselves has been the hallmark of strong teachers everywhere. To recognize how students learn and to engage them in the learning (versus the knowing) process is a crucial undertaking. When students emerge from classrooms as confident learners, when they can point to the results of their discoveries and the products of their achievements, there is no task that will daunt their perceived ability to undertake it. Students will be able because of their own experience pursuing knowledge rather than doing it as a result of the imperatives of teachers and "the curriculum." Some teachers and students may still *choose* not to learn; these folks will "jump" on command, do the report for a grade. On the other hand, many more students and teachers, having the courage to learn, will dimply dive in! A 'd' verb in a community of care, energy, and delight!

J   Juxtapose!

Phew! I can be a bit much, for sure! That was a long one, and it wasn't even a story! As a result, I think all that needs saying here is that teachers have two, often apparently conflicting responsibilities, classroom instruction – and everything else laid on top of that by local, state, and federal expectation.

"If wishes were horses, then beggars would ride…." I think it is time to put wishing and wanting aside. Some things may not – and perhaps should not – change. I simply suggest putting the teaching-learning teacher-student dynamic side by side and compare the goals for each. Fundamentally, I think the roles for each are ever more similar than separate. On top of that, our roles as advocates for the learning and doing we value and believe in cannot stop; we cannot stop attempting to be advocates for change. Understanding our full role will eliminate barriers that enable – and sometimes even nurture – the status quo.

We are more like our students than we care to admit. We have simply long ago learned the lessons of conformity to rules, cultural norms, and expectations; that's called being an adult! We may not be able to change the first two, but we can change the expectations because we do the work we expect our students to do, that is, we put in the time on their work, we explore what we don't know as a result of their work, and we move forward, bringing them forward, together. I suspect more than ever teachers are working in this way. As for the other, the things that don't change, certain 'rules' for example? Teachers who are learners have to ask *why not* and construct a "lesson plan," and then another, and another that incrementally but continuously build the change we seek. Juxtapose what is with what could be; thinkers like Finkel (2000), Kuhn (2005), Langer (1997), and Postman (1995) offer fuel to fire your thinking. They and many others make what might feel impractical or out of reach into something exciting to contemplate and possible to accomplish.

1994

| K | **Knowledge** |

Gosh, yes, you have to know something! I want a doctor who knows a lot of specialized information, and I want a lawyer who knows how to protect my interests. I want a plumber who knows how to fix the well and a contractor who builds my house "plumb."

To "know your stuff" is critical. *Knowing what stuff to know* is more critical. Believing in the power of learning and the courage it takes to pursue and assess it is most critical. That belief places a value on learning, which incorporates knowing, not as the final end point but as a place to take a breath, to stop a moment "for now." Expertise is acquired thought through the pursuit of specialized knowledge. The ability to assess which experts to call upon, when, requires a different type of expertise. Perhaps, if we held a curious mind in greater esteem than we currently do, and perhaps if we valued our own critical capacities to learn more highly, we would tolerate less "junk" in almost every aspect of our lives. Ahh, there's a 'j' word! We would be out and about, finding out, rather than sitting down, passively listening, and being told.

2020

Knowledge, continued

Having recently completed an articulate and fascinating biography about Alexander von Humboldt (Wulf, 2015), I finally realize what is so captivating about knowledge to me. I am curious about how the scientist, the writer, the explorer, the historian, the poet, came to be. As a young girl, I used to read all the biographies I could get my hands on. I wanted to know who these people were, what influenced them, how they made decisions and what those were. Why were they so brave, so committed, so determined, so sure, it seemed? Why did it seem so *easy* for them?

I think our "job," beyond teaching math and science, events and language, is to suggest 'journey.' Our students aren't hardly begun when we meet them and aren't hardly done when they leave us. What they are, however, at *whatever* moment, is *on their way*. Weeks, semesters, quarters, exams, and grade levels are arbitrary systems set up to make the trail, like heading West, accessible to the masses. And then we read of genius, who doesn't make it through high school, or genius, who enters college at the age of twelve. Such individuals are on their own journeys; they are courageous enough to go against the grain, to step off the trail. My students always knew things I did not; my appreciation for new forms of music, ideas in science, moments in history, all kinds of sports, experiences of other cultures and genders grew from trying to grasp my learners' individual journeys.

Experienced teachers know how much work teaching is – a caring teacher is always listening, asking questions, finding out and often holding what they learn dear, whether to ask about later or to bring in another for consult or support. As I remember listening to teacher talk beyond the everyday, I often heard themes underneath such as love; challenge; concerns and legitimate frustrations with underlying policies or structure; satisfaction with clear and thoughtful leadership. Teachers live their own journeys in the embrace of learning with their students, a different – and often more motivating – hold than that of curriculum, grade level, and progress.

So, I guess I am asking teachers who are reading this to hold in a place of honor all you have come to know, appreciate, and deal with. It is more than is asked of those from any other profession, because the days are never done, and the process *isn't* simply 9 to 3 with 6 weeks of summer vacation. There is research out there, oral histories of teachers' lives. Honor yours! It matters more than you may ever know, and it matters all the same. What you know, what you think about beyond your "major" and your "curriculum," is vast. Use your mind! As my mom would say, "Stand up straight!" Be proud of yourself and what you are accomplishing in the living/learning that is your working life.

1994

| L | There are 5 "l" words, all priorities:

Living, Loving, Learning (= work = fun) **Laughing, Listening**

2020

The 5 Ls

As I look at these concepts, words on the page, I know why I left the space beneath unfilled so many years ago. It is simply because what I have come to understand about any of these things doesn't really matter. What matters is *your* living, loving, learning (which is work and fun), your laughing and listening. That you are there. That you care. Experience is a noun for all the actions you undertake. With experience comes wisdom. With wisdom comes a sense of calm, and ease, and confidence in the toughest moments with the most challenging situations. Learning teachers don't think "been there, done that." They consider the context and quickly assess if what they are seeing *is* the same thing as past experience or something rather slightly different, given the individual in front of them. Every child, no matter how similar to one in age and height and temperament to another in the past, *is not that child*. Each deserves the 'l' words, because for him or her, it is the very first time they have met you…and you, them.

Hmm. Don't mean to be preachy, although I undoubtedly come by it honestly. Dad used to go on about "whatever" at the dinner table; we called it "the sermon." We went to church as a family; I sat through two services each Sunday because I was in the choir. So, I listened a lot (until another choir member brought a book under her robe to read during the second service; and then there were two of us doing so!). I also had an uncle who was a missionary overseas, although my dad was sure his oldest brother was with the CIA!

I just care so darned much – even, ever still – about the work teachers and learners, learners all, do. Our work makes us better, bigger, stronger, more capable; it makes us powerful. It is awe-inspiring as achievements abound.

A few months ago, I read an article in the local paper about a former advisee of mine. Ross aspired to be an elementary teacher from the beginning of his college career, a goal he has since successfully accomplished. He was in two of my classes, and although there were moments of "shine," he never seemed terribly interested. 'Just wait,' he told me, more than once. 'Just wait. You'll see.'

I did see. I was able to observe his student teaching, and I was blown away by his "flow." I think his mom was a teacher; I think he had a little brother. I *know* there was a lot I never knew about Ross, but he enacted these five concepts during that semester and has been doing so ever since. The elementary school where he student-taught hired him upon graduation. I was reading about him in the paper because he was recently recognized as an outstanding educator. Ross *was* the 'l' words, quietly, when I was knowing him. He is living them still, out loud. From what I have seen of this COVID19 spring when teachers are mentioned with great appreciation and respect, I suspect you, too, are living the 'l' words more than ever. Please stay healthy, strong, and positive; you are necessary, *essential* workers! You may not make the papers, but that does not mean you aren't vital to the work.

1994

M Meaning

Because I cannot use "chocolate" as the 'm' word, I will select the concept of meaning, which is something we don't usually "make" alone. What is "meaningful" to me may not be to you. I cannot assume my class is a meaningful experience for all 36 students all of the time. I cannot be sure the activities I select for them will foster their ability to understand. I must try. I prepare, I think about, I redo, I imagine, I finally plan.

When I first conceptualized this book, I wanted to make something of "meaning." I think it is probably true for most of us; we can imagine more – or different, and perhaps better as we understand things – than what it is we actually do or are asked to do. I think sometimes it is easy to feel diminished and unimportant in the greater scheme of things. Yet, *in* the greater scheme of things, we aren't even a known quantity. However, we *are* a known quantity to our family and friends, to our students, colleagues, and neighbors. Because we have working minds, hearts, and spirits, because we give others time, attention, thought, and energy, meaning is possible. No one else's definition will matter. Who you are among your "known" *is* known.

Pondering the possible is what teachers do every single moment, it seems. Our lives are full of meaning given the work we have chosen; our days are spent among others in interaction and decision making. Teaching is a *career* of making meaning; choosing it commits one to a full and meaning-full life.

M & Ms are an 'em' word, too, aren't they? I know what they mean to me!

2020

M Magnanimity

Although I can barely pronounce this word, it fits here, in the middle of the alphabet, in the middle of thinking about learning and teaching and being. And because this is one letter whose "modern" version I had not yet written, I choose this word to express what I am seeing on the news, hearing on the radio, and reading in the local paper. A definition stated something about a "largeness and generosity of temperament." Magnanimity is a quality teachers exemplify. It is a quality currently expressed by many, many more individuals around the world who are either helping others in their work as health care workers/support services or who acknowledge that work and volunteer to support the elderly, youth, and small businesses in their communities. As a nation, we are showing it is our want, our desire, to be magnanimous. To remain open is a capacity that can be grown. Generosity of spirit can also be grown even during these trying times, while knowing teaching *is* trying at times in the best and worst meaning of the word. I see it all around. I am humbled by "we, the people."

1994

| N | **Notice**

I think I mean this word as an imperative. Notice! Look up! I wrote a story a while ago, a summary of impressions and feelings that piled up like stones used to fill the pot holes in the drive. Only this time, they fill the hole and stack up higher and higher. I cannot ignore them, go around them or run them over. I must attend to them, these mulitple knowings that have no words, but leave an impression like a cookie stamp upon my mind or heart. I know I notice; seems to be what I do.

Notice! and look up!

2012

| N | **Narrate**

I am a researcher who prefers story-telling, or narrative, to statistics. In order to do the one, however, I had to learn the other. I had to understand the stories numbers can tell to better learn what they leave out. Only by understanding statistics was I able to appreciate the power of language and story to "get at" what the numbers cannot address. Many research studies today utilize both statistical and narrative processes to describe what happens in classrooms.

Two of the biggest arguments against narrative are a) it takes too long, and b) not all the information gained is "relevant," depending upon who is doing the reading. However, the connection between reading and writing and learning and thinking is known. On the other hand, one of the biggest arguments against statistics is that the "language" of numbers does not always point to the 'real' issue of concern. Regardless, I think there is value in each.

The first narrator I remember hearing was the voice on the record "Peter and the Wolf." Since then, I always tried to read aloud whenever I could in order to hear the words, not just compute them through the eyes into the brain. I have not been in a classroom in 5 years; do kids still read out loud? Do teachers read them stories? Do they read to each other? In a world full of sounds, with such easy access to all things digital, are students better readers? Better listeners? Would you think yes? Or no? Hmm. I could review the recent research, which I have not done. I think I was a better thinker when I was learning in harmony with others.

I wonder what your story is, and I wonder how it influences your teaching and learning? It took a college student to finally help me understand something I never knew was an issue for me. One year in the mid-90s, among nineteen freshmen taking a Foundations of Education class, I had one particularly bright young woman who had a mouth on her that went beyond acceptable in any classroom. I asked her to watch her language. I had stopped her after a class and reminded her again. Things went well for a bit and then one day, the ^&%*# poured out of her. I turned from the rest of the group, called her by name, and sternly said something like, "That's enough. Please leave the classroom and come back when you can keep your language in check." Then, as she told me later that morning, I simply turned back to the rest of the class like nothing had happened and continued to work through the discussion we were having.

She waited outside the classroom. I asked if she had time to meet, and she did. We sat, me in a low chair, she in a slightly higher one, both away from the desk. No doubt I started off with something like, "What *is* it? Why this language, when you know better?"

While trying to maintain her composure – she had been crying some – she asked me instead, "Dr. Meloy, you tell *me* what it is!"

"What do you mean?" I asked her. She replied: "You are so nice, we want to please you so, but then something like this happens, and you turn so cold and impersonal and mean. Why do you *do* that?"

Okay, I am thinking. I *do* that? The moisture in my eyes was starting to build as I thought about my reactions to her behavior. The first thing I understood, and then tears *did* start to fall, was that her perception of my behavior was painfully accurate. On one level, I could have said to her with ease and confidence in my position as teacher: 'Of course, why would I disrupt any more of my class? Of course I'd "go back" to 'who I was' as you say, because 'she' never left; I never raised my voice, that's who I am.' I knew that reply would get me nowhere in understanding what this young woman meant. "How can you change like that?" she asked again while I sat there thinking as fast as I could, "Why did you *do* that?" she pressed.

Of course, when I figured it out – and I did – it hit me like a ton of bricks! It would have been so easy (and safe) for me to be defensive and tell her it was *her* behavior that set me off, it was *her* fault, but as soon as those words – or words like them – formed in my head, I knew that wasn't what she meant. She meant, where did that behavior come from, not today, because today her behavior was a trigger, but rather in *my* past. What event/experience shaped *my* unconscious and automatic response to her? As soon as I understood the question, it was as if my father were standing in front of me, telling me never to use that language again while marching me to the bathroom to wash my mouth out with soap. *Dial* soap. (I was 5! I didn't even know what I had said!) Some 40 years later, I responded to this young, bright, woman as my father had responded to me, never questioning if I knew what I was saying or if my response was appropriate. As soon as I had resolved the issue as my dad had done, I could automatically "switch back," like he did, to the 'good' dad/teacher. Like it never happened. Really, Judy? You have buttons that can be pushed???

All of this went through me in a flash; I was trying hard to understand, as quickly as I could. And as I began to explain what I think had happened, what was the real issue between us, I was crying, too, just as she was. I identified foul language as a "button" for me that she had unknowingly "pushed."

Wow! Talk about insight into one's own behavior! I thanked her for helping me to understand what had happened between us. She apologized for her part, because she *had* heard me in the classroom earlier, and in the hallway at a later time; she *knew* she shouldn't swear, and she had been trying. And that is what also upset her so, *the fact she had been trying* while my response did nothing to acknowledge this fact. Hadn't she in fact improved? Did she have to be perfect right then, now and forever?

Phew. I learned so much from her that day. Patience is a 'p' word, understanding is a 'u' word, but I needed to consider the whole of my work with college students related to their *journey*, not their perfection, which is a huge concept. I needed to reconsider all courses, with all students. What I learned that day was the young people I have in my classroom are as "senior" as they have ever been; they are as old/mature/adult as they have ever been. Older than yesterday, just like each of us. I needed to understand the 'now' between us and not assume, which I obviously had, that learning *was* a light switch. We often don't get things right the first time; duh! I knew this, and yet that is *not* how I responded. Messing up "again" does not automatically mean someone is a bad or a poor learner; it does not mean the teacher hasn't been heard or the student isn't listening. It simply meant on that day, I expected a "right answer" and her behavior generated a "pat" and incorrect response from me. From that day on, I remembered this "ah hah" when about to respond "automatically" to another student; with a moment's hesitation and thought, I think I was better able to respond to the learning happening before me in the moment, at least I sincerely hope so. A deeper question still remained, however: Judy, when do you get in your own way?

That day I learned not only about this young woman, where she was 'coming from' and why she responded in certain ways, which she explained, but also about myself, from my own story, something so internalized I was totally unaware there was anything "wrong" about my behavior. I am forever grateful to JB for her courage and openness with me that day. Our stories – even ones we no longer listen to – are a part of us. This one needed to be uncovered, shown the light of day, culled for what might be kept and the rest taken to the dump! I do love living in Vermont, don't you?

1994

☐O☐ Opportunity

Living is an opportunity. Teaching is an honor and a chance to learn more.

Learning is an opportunity, to know more, do more, be more.

Listening to others enhances opportunities to learn, think, and feel.

Loving is an opportunity; it means being vulnerable and open to the lives and thoughts of others.

Laughing is an opportunity. Sharing smiles and good will is so critical in this most serious world.

Opportunities abound. Education *is* an opportunity, and it generates others. Some teachers blast their way into unknown territories, and students follow behind with their cave lights. Some teachers whisper, "the power is yours," and students look around to see if they heard correctly. Some teachers inspire, others conspire, all teachers – those anywhere in our lives – believe in "opportunity." They hope for the best, and in the best of who we are as learners and what we can become. Or so I will take this opportunity to believe. Don't you?

2006

☐O☐ Ordinary

Judy, don't be!

2020

PS

    Never give empty space to someone who hates to waste paper and who loves taking a pencil to a blank page. In 2020, there is a commercial on TV for an exercise bike; the dad is on the bike, the trainer is encouraging him, "Go for it, don't be mediocre!" His young daughter, maybe 5, is watching him. As he finishes getting ready for work and puzzles with his tie, the young girl is standing in the doorway and says, "Come on! Don't be mediocre!"

    I think that is what is wrong with the concept of "average." I am not sure the two terms are equivalent. No doubt we have heard the statement, "I can do nothing and still pass," or "That's good enough." Nowhere have I talked about expectations, or even more necessarily asked the question, why have them? Why ask kids to work harder – what is the value, and who's value? Then I notice the piano in the living room, my biggest dust catcher. Being neither Beethoven nor Alicia Keyes doesn't mean I can't enjoy playing, when enjoyment is the goal: not mastery, expertise, or even commitment.

    I remember suggesting to my last group of incoming transfer students, when they questioned the lack of one clear guideline ensuring them they would get an A in the class, that it was easy to be mediocre. Anybody can be. But they chose to transfer, to have another shot of being *somebody* here. Being somebody requires more effort, on a consistent basis; it requires self-understanding and self-love/appreciation; it requires commitment. Athletes tend to know this because they are a part of a team; they do not want to let the team down. What is happening now? Have teachers formed teams to share new ideas, think through solutions, and create possibilities, or has COVID19 made colleagueship even more difficult? If learning is no longer ordinary, can it still be mediocre, an 'm' word for not good enough? But that is *my* value. What's yours? And if you don't want to work hard, every day, for the rest of your working life, *why* would you *ever* choose teaching as a career? "Loving children" is not a strong enough reason, because if you are *not* working for them, their families, and your community with "above average" persistence and devotion every day your physical, mental, and emotional health allows, then you *aren't* truly loving them, are you?

1994

P Power

The real world of college classrooms still has the teacher's desk in front and the student desks facing it. I was talking with one of my students yesterday about that image. I told her as I looked out "at the 36 of you," that they, the students, were the front of my classroom. Kate listened, respectfully, but with visible uncertainty as to my meaning.

What was clear in the ensuing discussion was that I sounded a little crazy! I have enough experience with preservice teachers that as soon as they come to the desk in front of a room, their posture changes, their attitude about what they know and don't know changes, their "sense of authority" changes. They try to be the "knowers," the "experts" on the topic they have prepared. They know information is being collected on how well they present as well as on the substance of what they present. They are aware of themselves as "teachers" rather than as learners. The power emanating from that place in the room is unbelievable; the confidence it gives them is easily observable. What happens next, though, is a funny thing. The students deliver, often not at all as they have been taught in a preservice methods course, but usually as they have experienced teaching throughout their lives and in the majority of their other college classrooms. Hmm.

One current notion of power is that the most powerful leader is the one who gives power away. In college classrooms, the idea of the professor taking a seat in the back row is, I suspect, uncommon. For example, I rarely "leave my post" at the front of the room. I can blame it on the classroom configuration and the numbers of students, but the opportunities for me to weave in and around all of my college students as they interact with the day's material is limited. Even if I were sitting with them in a circle, I could still lecture; I could still be the voice of authority. As the students seem to expect it, power "obviously" resides not only in *my* location in the room, but also in *my* knowledge – of content, direction for the day, purposes for actions. The receivers of those decisions wait with notebooks open and pencils poised. They are "ready to learn." So, what's the point? Do I not practice what I preach?

The role of teacher is continually changing. It is being described with such terms as mentor, coach, facilitator, co-learner, co-inquirer, collaborator. In my classroom, I suspect the students still view me as the knower, with power over their futures even as I work to empower them to make decisions about how much they will do and how hard they will work to do it. We complete regular self-assessments; the word must be out I don't suffer fools gladly, because the students are ever better at candid self-appraisal. By the end of the semester, they know what they have earned; they know what they have chosen to do…and not do. They can look at their own awareness of the tasks completed, opportunities maximized and arrive at a fair evaluation based upon the evidence before them. I may have the power position, but the power of the grade rests in their minds and accomplishments, and finally, their pens. And they know it in conscious ways.

My hope is that these aspiring teachers become better able to understand their own efforts – and lack of them – as they pursue their teaching careers; that they become unwilling to do less than their best because they know they could be doing more; that the concept of "the average teacher" does not mean a mediocre one. I hope aspiring teachers have learned what they are capable of. I hope they became grabbed by the need to learn in order to *be* their best, rather than by the need to know so as to prove they *are* the best.

Both needs motivate. I often have to do my homework because I need to know something in order to be better prepared for tomorrow. The need to know and the ability to act on that need are hallmarks of enabled learners and productive teachers. As much contemporary writing suggests, the teaching-learning process is more reciprocal and integrated than ever suggested before. Perhaps when students believe they have the power to learn, when they are honored not solely for the amount of their learning but for the process and paths their learning takes, their success – perhaps their knowledge "found" – is something that will not be forgotten after the test, and their abilities to discover more will not be limited to the topic at hand.

I don't know if the above is true or even possible. At the moment, I see students for 3 of 38 credits in education and that same number over the 128 credits they need to graduate. The force of prior learning and their growing up in classrooms grades K-12 is a power beyond measure. But I am hopeful. I struggle to enact and enable a different type of confidence in my classrooms. I believe in the ability of my students to go beyond whatever I can teach them. I believe in our power as teachers to motivate and enable *learners*. I believe, beyond whatever energy I generate as my "power," that the power important to generate is *theirs*, for the future of all of us.

2020

P Power

I did not know Kuhn's book until 2008, fourteen years after I wrote the first draft of this book. As you have read, I, in the present tense, have questioned my own statements and assumptions made when I thought I knew what I was thinking, knowing, and doing. So, I will sound like so many authors I have read when I state: When students believe they have the power to learn, when they are honored not solely for the amount of their learning but also for the process and paths their learning takes, their success/their knowledge "found" is something that will not be forgotten after a test; their abilities to discover more will not be limited to the topic at hand. "Authentic assessment" has been around for years, as has the emphasis on how answers are derived, although only as the exception in the early to mid-1990s.

Back in 1994, I *did* have a sense about the power of the processes required to grasp and hold onto information, the building toward knowledge. I knew classrooms were changing even then – whole language, authentic assessments, and later project-based learning and cooperative learning, and, near the end of my tenure at Castleton, constructivist learning and critical pedagogy.

I am not saying I discovered anything. In 1994, I had never heard of Deanna Kuhn (2005) or Ellen Langer (1997). I am only commenting that by having documented what I was thinking – and now looking at it years later when additional "history" has been made in schools related to learning and teaching – I can simply assert what we probably all take for granted: teaching is a thinking act as much as learning is, because as much learning comes from it as from external sources themselves. For example, journal writing was a big deal in the beginning of the 21st century. For licensure, students developed portfolios, where they, too, had to reflect on their recent learning and document where their thinking and understandings had changed. Writing is a *power*ful tool, utilizing "work," "energy," and "narrative." Castleton preservice secondary students learned this from Drs. Ron Savage and Judy Miller, who taught "Reading and Writing in the Content Area." I even taught one section of this course early on and learned a lot.

I am grateful to still be alive. I am grateful to live in Vermont, especially during these COVID19 days. That I can continue to think and grow means I am living forward, into today. It is not necessarily true that old teachers leave and just fade away. To this day, I know I carry with me fragments of what I learned from them – cognitively, emotionally, and intuitively. I am grateful and thank them for fostering me, guiding me, challenging me, and respecting me; for leading my learning forward. Mrs. Pate, Mr. Woodhouse, Mrs. Fletcher, and professors Ilse Winter, Helen Frye, Stephen Ball, David Clark, Don Cunningham, Egon Guba, and many others' chosen work made possible my own. Thank you.

1994

Q Quit

I am a quitter. I do not give up easily, I am persistent, but sometimes I choose not even to play the game. I quit before I start. Sometimes, it is easier to cry than to be tenacious, easier to pick up something else than to finish what I started. There. I have said it, and it is the only "pity party" in this book. Have you seen the expression where you take the thumb of your hand and strum it across the face of your little finger on the same hand? It means, "the world's smallest violin." It is played when we hear someone whine or complain.

Let's face it; life isn't easy. There are no solutions that can't be challenged in retrospect. We hurt each other, intentionally and un-. We are careless and can act stupidly. We put ourselves first more often than not when it doesn't really matter, and when it counts, we don't assert ourselves enough. We don't believe. We quit. We excuse ourselves. We are only human after all: I won't apply myself; who would notice? Nobody cares. I am tired.

As I have reached "middle age," I recognize ever more clearly that life is a ratio of days lived over total number of days. The problem is, since we cannot jump into the future or stand in the past, the ratio of days to total days we are living in any given moment is one. Today is the only day we have, no matter how we plan, and hope, and wish. Now is the only moment we have to be our best. If we quit now, what does that leave us for tomorrow? A little less of ourselves. A little less of our ability and our dreams. I want my life to represent a whole number. You deserve my presence and my best in this moment, because I cannot guarantee you another. So, I listen well. Takes energy. I plan well. Takes energy. I interact, as best I can. I teach, I learn, I read, I love my family. I try to do these things well. Takes energy. I can't quit these things today and then pick them back up tomorrow as if nothing happened. You won't know it of me today if I promise I will try to do it tomorrow, and I then I don't. I am not saying we can't slow ourselves down, or that we must give our all to everything all of the time; the former is wise and the latter is hardly sane! However, when you are with your students, your "kids" or young children, in that time they deserve the best you are; prioritizing sleep, family, and preparation so that you can be your best in that day of now is all I mean. Don't quit on *them*. Or you!

We will all be done, soon enough. But the beautiful energy, life, laughter, belief, opportunity, and hope that is yours needs to be lived today, in this moment, with your students. As difficult as it is. I can't quit. I can do things "the easy way," or I can be a learning teacher. I *can* quit, but if I do, be sure to kick me out of your school!! The kids, colleagues, parents, and community deserve better. There are plenty of easy jobs, but teaching is a constant work in progress. Leave it to those of us committed to caring about the lives we meet, willing to do the work of it while being open to the lessons we learn along the way.

2020

Q Query

My neighbor down the lane called a few minutes ago. Robin is a retired lawyer from Connecticut and a special human being. We differ in politics, and we are both entranced with the nature outside our doors. She paints, I write; she has a dog, I an old cat. The other day, she asked how I was doing? Like she was, I suspected. We both live in solitude but our freedoms were not restricted until March of this year. Living now is different for everyone.

She asked, *what* are you doing? I told her this long-time project needed to be finished and then explained. I concluded by saying: 'I think the remaining letters will go more quickly. I mean, who uses a 'q' word, right?' She laughed and then suggested quietly, "Query?" Yes! Of course! I knew I had used the word "question" throughout some of the earlier letters, but when she said it, query sounded more, well, just a bit special. So here is the 'q' word: query.

As a transitive verb, query means to question something, especially if you are not sure it is correct (Collins, online dictionary). To me, that sounds like a serious question. Perhaps the most serious query I ever answered was "Why did you become a teacher?" That was something I had thought about for a long time.

Unlike some of my students, who entered college knowing they wanted to be a teacher and never wavered (I am thinking of Kate, for example, who ended up getting her license and heading to Africa for a year or two teaching with the Peace Corps), I never wanted to be a teacher. Too many people told me I "should" be one, which immediately turned my mind in other directions. It wasn't until I was out of college and working as a management trainee in a bank that I made the decision. I had been asked to develop a questionnaire for tellers to find out about their jobs, the work environment, etc. I hesitated, saying I had only had one psychology class, and I knew there were correct ways to form a questionnaire. I did not have that knowledge; I would have to study some first. I was told it didn't matter. Just do it.

While I was thinking about any real choice I might have, two things happened. First, my immediate boss was promoted on the handbook for the bank that I had initiated, pulled together, and subsequently written, the result of being handed thirty-two different colored pieces of paper as my "orientation packet." Second, my wallet was taken from my purse when I was summoned to his office so he could tell me about *his* success. I went home and decided what the bank thought was best for me and what I wanted to do with my time were two different things. I missed "kids." Somehow working with adults left me wanting – things weren't always what they seemed, the challenges didn't feel quite right, and the expectations were rather low. I quit my job, entered graduate school, took work as a waitress, and looked forward to substituting and then teaching. What was I, 25 or 26 when I got my first teaching job? (see letter 'a') Better late than never!

So then, it is here I thank my neighbor for providing the 21st century 'q' word. I am fine with questions, but this one, this query, probably matters more than I even understand. I am so happy I made the decision to go back to school to become a teacher. Teaching isn't easy, but it is work I chose to do and wanted to do, because it was work that kept me learning. What other jobs offer so many new opportunities every single day? Which means my query for you is: Why do you/did you want to be a teacher? Will it be/has it been good for you? Do you love learning? Will you be, or are you good for teaching? I have to ask, you know; I have an inquiring mind!

1994

R Recognition

Among the many 'r' words I considered, such as reward or revelry, I think the responsible word choice is probably recognition, but not in the sense of being held up to the light or compared to others. This word ties in with noticing, because what a teacher recognizes about him/herself and his/her students becomes the strength of the bridges built between them. Recognition means acknowledging one's limits, one's challenges, and one's abilities. Recognition has to do with not being falsely modest or unwarrantedly conceited. Recognition has to do with knowing about one's self, about "learning again." Recognition is supported by reflection. When I reflect upon what I do or say, I am sometimes able not only to recognize qualities I like in myself, but also qualities that may not be so praiseworthy (see 2012 letter 'n'). I can acknowledge my limits, my differences, and what I have in common with others. I am more aware of others as I am able to recognize me from and among them. Recognition enables graciousness toward the humanness of others; recognition enables passionate, vocal response when persons or ideas are maligned or abused. Recognition fosters further inquiry; it keeps me whole, knowing again, learning anew.

2020

> **R** Recognize!

I need to make this concept the verb it was meant to be. I can't help but think of the Irish blessing, about knowing what you can change, what you cannot, and understanding the difference…or is the blessing the one about having the wind at your back? I will have to check, but you-all probably know the saying better than I.

You-all. When I first began teaching, my middle schoolers in every class, 6th, 7th, and 8th, asked me, "WHY do you say "you-all" all of the time? Are you from the South?!" I still smile as I think of them. I explained that unlike the German language, which has two words for "you," singular and plural, we only use the one word in English. "I can say You, meaning you, Beth, or I can say YOU and look around the classroom and mean all of you. Although I do have a niece and two nephews in Texas, and they are about your age, and they DO say "you-all", I use it in English so you all know I am talking to you – all!"

So, who are *you*? Where are you from? Let me know you a bit, says the student. Tell me who you are. It matters. You matter.

At a time when we are hearing so much of 'virtual' this and that, give me something real, something authentic, something/someone I can look in the eye. I hope it will end, because the work of teaching and learning requires empathy, understanding, and interactions with adults other than our parents or family members; it thrives in places where facts have context, can be queried, noticed, and "looked up." When work is done together, hands-on, "minds-on," it feels less *like* work. For this to happen, I need to learn the challenges and subsequent conclusions of what *you all* have come to recognize in the spring of COVID19. I know each of you can tell me.

*1994/**2020***

$\boxed{S}$ Sympathy (the old-timey definition)

I obviously had something in mind when I wrote the place holder, above. Yet, there are no clues in the several files holding versions of this book. I had to go to the trusty on-line dictionaries to fill in the blank.

From the Merriam Dictionary on line: "The difference in meaning is usually explained with some variation of the following: **sympathy** is when you *share* the feelings of another; **empathy** is when you understand the feelings of another *but do not necessarily share them"* (italics are mine). I think this definition is close to what I was trying to explain, but I checked another source for further clarification. The Old Oxford English dictionary offers a second definition, or the same one put another way: **sympathy** is "an *understanding* between people; common feeling." It is the notion of understanding I was getting at, not "shared feelings."

I think many teachers, regardless of grade level or content, have sympathy for each other in this way. We share experiences bigger than a child vomiting on the floor or a student showing up tardy again. Of course, we share these things, too! We know about learning and conditions that get in its way, things often beyond our control. We know about work. We know about pain and sorrow, our children's and our own. We know the need of routine for many and variety for others even as we desire respect for *our* efforts, such as trying something new or explaining something more than once in a different way, while simultaneously maintaining some level of sympathy for the efforts of our colleagues. As teachers, regardless of age and experience level, we share so very much in common. Sometimes, we don't see it that way, especially when our personal interests are at stake. But in its ideal form, sympathy is much like the nation's and our state's current mantra: "We are all in this together." Except, of course, when we are not. Sympathy, the "old-timey" notion, is probably both needed and appreciated more than ever.

2020 PS

Sharing

Maybe the 's' word should be "safe," but learning is hardly, ever, safe. It is disruptive, challenging to what is held secure. It can be dis-confirming and is often confusing. That school buildings and classrooms should be safe goes without saying. We all have been hurt by gun violence and attitudes toward it and inactions surrounding it. Perhaps we are all 'safer' now that schools are not open? Perhaps learning is flourishing differently, but more independently? How do we grow learners now, through the screen? How do we provide the support and critique, the success and the challenge, the kudos and the questions? What happens when your – or their – computer fails, if they have one at all? What happens when interest flags, yours and theirs? Why am I thinking of "Dora the Explorer" or the crazy Ms. Frizzle? It is not school as usual. What are we creating *now* that needs to be in place when we return? Which routines have been jarred? What exciting things are working now that never would have emerged in the configuration of your classroom? I bet you are thinking about these things. Are you writing them down, or sharing them with colleagues and friends? Please do. We, the public, the teacher educators, need to learn from you. Gain sympathy for your ideas, for the passions that have emerged during this pandemic. Maybe the 's' word should have been "sharing"? I like this idea very much.

PS: Again! Just in case you were wondering, I will answer a question asked so long ago: **No**. I never was a cheerleader… but I cheer learners, always!

1994

T Trust

Someone has written that there are two main ways to talk about trust. Some of us start out trusting others until trust is broken; others of us wait to see if trust can be placed in someone. I don't recall in this discussion anyone talking about trusting ourselves.

In earlier "letters" I have talked about the courage required of learners and the confidence taking a "learning" rather than a "teaching" stance requires. As I think about my students, I see many who have not learned to trust themselves and their abilities. They seem to place their trust in me, their teacher, their advisor, as someone who has "been there, done that." I am not suggesting their trust is misplaced. Mentors are needed; knowledge needs to be disseminated. I *am* suggesting that by the time I see them, they have had at least 20 years of learning experience behind them. I would think they would be extremely confident in their ability to learn by now.

Part of the difficulty, it seems to me, is their desire either to please me because I am the teacher, or to do as little as possible in order to see how I will respond. In both cases (extreme ones, to make a point), their actions are not grounded in their own sense of well-being as learners. I miss students I have never had even as I miss many whom I have met. I miss not having in my classroom the student who wants to proceed with a topic or idea that was briefly covered in class. I miss the student who, upon reflecting in his/her journal, chooses to inquire about where he/she can get more information. I miss the student who says, "I was just reading about this; I think it pertains to class, can we talk about it a little?" I miss students who recognize the limitations of their learning or who want to break out beyond the borders of the content areas we have framed.

I do have a student or two who brings in an article related to class. I do have a student or two who writes more questions than answers in journal entries and with whom I dialogue. I do have many more students who are committed to their goal to become teachers. I simply see few students who are yet of the age or inclination to understand the ramifications of their choices; I see few students who trust their ability to make choices for themselves beyond those in their prescribed programs.

I am being unfair. Many colleges and universities are adopting a 5th year program. Students complete a bachelor's degree and then pursue their interest in teaching in a master's program. These students are older and have a solid liberal arts degree behind them. In our state, the costs of higher education would preclude many students from becoming teachers were a 5th year program the only option.

For me, the point is simply this. The average student in my classroom is a capable learner. He/she can do the assignments, well. He/she can do what is expected, well. I expect more! Seems to me I am putting something on the students that may not yet be a value of theirs? Perhaps I am asking, "Why isn't it?"

Hmm. If I *am* asking, then maybe it is *I* who needs to trust? When I think of past graduates about whom I have some knowledge, five immediately come to mind: Jackie, Dana, Kristen, Scott and Darren. Then there's Betsy, Leah, Kim, Rob, and Patty…. Maybe I am just longing to be back in the classrooms of inspired and capable learners? Maybe I am just fighting a stereotyped educational system? Maybe it is simply the realization that I have no actual means of knowing what learning the majority of students I have met will use in their futures? Who will they be as teachers, or whatever path they choose? Perhaps it is *I* who must learn to trust, to acknowledge this "not knowing" is okay. They will be okay and most likely better than that! If I practice the ABCs I preach, then chances are the students with whom I have had the opportunity to think and learn have found something of my efforts and those of my colleagues worthwhile, to the benefit of themselves and the lives of children with whom they interact. To some extent, it is true that college kids, master's and doctoral students are less likely than my former 6th graders to acknowledge our role with a hug, but I must trust what I have learned with them and have come to understand about what they comprehend. Teaching is an act of faith, a sincere "believe." Come on, Judy, believe it!

2001, **December**

Trust, revisited (*abridged*, 2020)

When I returned in September after a year's leave of absence, my upperclass students seemed to have a case of 'nerves.' After a few sessions, we dealt with it directly. Although I finished that class calmly, I ended up heading to see the associate dean, who hadn't left for the day. He listened as I tried to work through what was happening. I wasn't sure whose issue it was; I wasn't sure what was going on. I only knew they were terribly uncomfortable. I dreaded heading back to class 46 ½ hours later. I didn't know how to say, "I wish you could sense and feel what I see as I look out at you." I wanted them to tell me how to help, but I wasn't even sure 'help' was the right notion. Something was between us. I felt a tremendous lack of trust; students seemed fearful, as if bracing themselves for whatever I was going "to do" to them. I was teaching fearful students. I know I don't learn well when I am afraid; I don't think anyone does.

I asked myself, what do *I* do when I feel this way? I turn to authors whose words have always inspired me. I sought out poetry and short speeches that revive the good, the possible, the believe in me. And then I wondered, if these words make *me* feel stronger, could they have a similar impact on my students?

I prepared for class by draping an old linen tablecloth around my shoulders like a monk's robe. After the class had been in the room for about 5 minutes, I walked in, saying nothing. There were a few snickers, a few smiles, and some faces of stone. Then I read to them – about courage; about knowing one's own mind and heart; about civil disobedience, strength, passion of spirit, and peace. Ten minutes later, I closed the books and walked out of the room, dropping the cloth outside the door. I reentered, apologizing for keeping them waiting. "I got held up," I said. "I hope you had something to think about while I was gone." Although they looked at me rather quizzically, their shoulders relaxed; their eyes were making contact with mine. We got to work. After class, a few students hung out just to say, "See ya Thursday." A few others arrived early to the next class and actually greeted me. I could sense they were still uncertain, but all seemed more confident in me and our working relationship; they were going to give us a try.

In conclusion, trust is bigger than me having it 'for you' or you deciding to grant it 'to me.' It requires an environment where actions are consistent, moments are linked, and human beings are valued.

2010; 2020

Trust is a Keeper!

Trust. Let it stand as is. Fledglings fly away, there is a new batch next year. A new opportunity, to *be* new, to renew, and to believe. It is worth it, the work we do. I have to trust the aspiring teachers, their forming values, their thinking practice. I only ever want them to live healthy, thriving, lives, so to benefit the lives of others. All the same, as every teacher can tell you, letting them go is often so much easier said than done. Little heart breakers, aren't they? No matter their age! We work hard, because we want them to make it, to be that much better prepared for the world outside their doors. We want them to make it! We work to make that aspiration a reality.

*1994; **2020***

| U | Understanding | V | Validity |

In 1994, I only had place holders for these two letters on the same page. In **2020**, I can only explain my lack of attention to them by their placement at the end of the alphabet! My heart is in this book a little bit; I think these letters didn't emerge as readily as the others.

I can only assume the 'u' word would end up being "understanding." That I did not type it in suggests it was too easy – and too difficult – a choice. As for the 'v' word, if former students from my first years at Castleton would have anything to suggest, no doubt they would offer "validity," in unison. They did *not* like the concept, but when they passed the testing/ assessment portion of the National Teacher's Examination, they were thrilled. "I knew EVERYTHING, Dr. Meloy!"

I was worried that these preservice teachers would think only of validity in terms of a reliable and valid oven, where chocolate chip cookies could turn out perfectly ONLY IF the oven temperature had been set at 350 degrees AND only *after* they had ascertained the oven held that temperature each time the dial was set. You see, their answers to short essays always referred to the term by relating the story of good cookies. After two semesters of seeing the same response, I *knew* I had more work to do, and maybe that is when and what I learned *to understand* about college teaching. Thanks to them, I continued to learn through my teaching in order to construct a more *valid* experience for us all; and yes, sometimes, I baked cookies, too 😊!

1994

| W | **Work = Learning = Fun**

Please flip back to the L words!

2020

PS

Thinking about Teaching and Learning has been/is Serious Fun!

Finalizing this volume took a different kind of work than that of creating it in the first place. My purpose in writing was to show what it is to learn by doing, when the doing is mind work. As you have read – unless you began at the back, which is something I often do with books – I learned while doing, and the doing lay learning bare. The "fun" is not this volume. It is/was the "all along the way," my years of teaching. In retrospect, even the tough parts, difficulties, and smallnesses of life among others in schools were a part of the "fun" hard work can be (I *still* have a huge yard to rake, and I still hear my father. I accomplish a task, and I learned by doing. And I smile).

I chose teaching, not because I *didn't* want to work, but because I *did*. And I wanted to work with kids, people who weren't totally formed and set in their ways of thinking and being. I chose teaching because I thought being committed to something – the learning, the students, the colleagues – seemed so very worth it to me. Yes, I was "young," and yes, I was idealistic. I am not sure I could approach learners any differently. To do less, to do the same thing year after year, would most certainly be one of the most boring jobs I can imagine, as it must have been for my high school history teacher (see 2020 'e')! The opportunity to learn something new every day, to be challenged, to become more patient, kind, and consistent, demanded more from me than "the average" work might have. It takes work to be better than mediocre, but the learning teaching requires is so worth it. Having held that value has made my teaching life truly fun. I hope you find it worth it as well, although I am not sure anyone can apply the word fun to this COVID19 spring. But I have no doubt you tried!

1994

☒ Marks the Spot!

The spot in teaching and learning is "time"; time to plan, to prep, to grade, to study, to do homework, to talk with a student, a parent, a colleague. Time away from all of those activities is a place of renewal; time to go to a soccer game, a senior recital, a play. We "spend" time helping with homework or driving through a snow storm with a young man who, at Thanksgiving time, had missed his bus to White River Junction. We "take" time to laugh with our colleagues just because. "X" marks the treasure, the pot of gold at the end of the rainbow. It is all of it that you are giving, have given your life to. It is your chosen profession.

On the limited number of TV channels I receive, there is a public information blurb about "the more you know." Often teachers are thanked, for noticing, encouraging, not forgetting, not accepting less than a student's best. In this case, "X" is not the *wrong* answer, but the *only* one.

Our students want our energy and our attention. They want us to believe in them and to notice them (noticing is the 'n' word). They want our time. It is the biggest gift a teacher can give a student. It is clearly a choice, to give time.

Sometimes, we make up an excuse. Sometimes, we have other priorities, and sometimes, we simply cannot be available. Students have their own lives, too, as we do. There are even times when they don't want us to notice them or offer time.

But when a student sees you in the audience of the first play he stars in or the first one she directs, when the soccer players smile as they come onto the field because you are smiling at them, when you encourage a young person to pursue their interest, that moment of time, of being interested in their ideas, their strengths, their lives, is a gift. Literally a present in the present. In "time."

Some want more of us than we can give. Some want less than our best. But deep down, kids simply know if they matter to teachers, because the teacher looks at them straight in the eyes, as if he/she were wearing an "X." You are in my sight and sound; I am thinking about *you* as I listen to your question. *You* are my priority at this moment, not something or someone else.

Teachers with families and home lives still make time and room for children, they still let kids know they are special. They still take the time to notice and believe. We only go around once. It is yours and theirs and "ours" together, this thing called time. For such an inexpensive offering – taking nothing from the paycheck or the holiday fund – the return is priceless, measured in memories and moments meaning more than perhaps we will ever know. Each moment a possibility; each breath a gift. X marks the spot! Time is the correct, and best, answer. Be present now, this one day. Be the treasure!

2020

Wanting Time

A long time ago, my first cat, Rama – meaning "Joy" – came upstairs to my desk and jumped on the keyboard, ruining the work on the page. He was middle-aged; he knew better. I gently, but firmly, tossed him aside. The next time I was at my desk, he tried the same thing, wondering, perhaps, if I had learned something in the interim. While removing my hand from the keyboard, I nudged it slightly to the left so he wasn't sitting directly on it. Then we just sat there. We talked a bit; I pet him some. After a while, I don't know how long, he jumped down.

An independent cat, he rarely asked for my attention. So, yes, I learned. Sometimes, others need to be first! Their way of asking may not always be appropriate or the way *we* would do things, but it does not mean we can't listen and be open for the 'teachable moment,' even when the tables seem turned and the learner is us! *

* I do know that nouns/pronouns on 'either side' of the verb "to be" are "subjects"; however, it feels so stilted to say, the learner is I, *or,* the learner is we. It's *us,* right?! Right!

1996

| Y | **Yes!**

I owe this word to my dear colleague, John Duval. Anyone who knows him understands how powerful a presence he is, as an educator and human being. We shared an office when I first arrived on campus, and we learned to stay out of each other's way; both of us being tall was a bit of an issue, but not an unpleasant one.

John's early work at Castleton took him to all corners of the state, even while completing his doctorate and managing a long commute. The Willie Nelson song, "On the Road Again" comes to mind, but I don't think I have ever heard him sing it.

What I learned from this man is something I was stubbornly unwilling to *ever* learn, because I didn't believe him. I did not think he was right. The issue between us? John always said "YES!" – I'll do it, I'll help you, I can find it, I'll call you, YES!

Really? To *everything* a student needed or wanted? Can you think the extension is necessary? Isn't that student just trying to test your limits? Isn't that grad student looking to "cop out" of completing residency? Yes, you know that, and yes, you think it's okay, and No, I don't think so, John. Not this time. NO. Did you really say, "Yes!"?

During the first three or four years of our knowing, I didn't pay much attention, but I knew he never denied a student's interest or request for help. No excuses. Only yes. By year two, I had my own office, and by year…was it 6 or 7, we had moved to a different building. Our offices were now right next to each other, which is when I paid more attention to this activity. Only recently did that little light bulb go off in my head.

I was working in the seating area outside the offices, spreading filing across the tables. A student was with John. They were talking, laughing, talking, and then, when finished up, the student left. I looked up.

I didn't tell you I had seen the person go *into* the office – the body language was that of a tired, somewhat uptight individual. When the individual walked out from John's office, I can only tell you this: it was *not* the same person. The tension was gone from the shoulders; the energy coming from him was tangible.

Okay, John, do you have a minute? Sure. Can I have a seat? Of course. What just happened? He explained the issue. I had heard similar ones before. He told me what he had suggested, how that suggestion was a "yes" and an eraser to the concerns the student was carrying. I looked at him, and I said: I think I finally get it. You may not be right, your response may not be "correct," but it *was* the right answer. I get it. You *are* right.

I am not being glib when I tell you I tried to think like John at some point during the following week, when an undergraduate who needed a "work around" came into my office to request one; what was needed was a solution that would get him where he needed to be, correctly, in the end, even if it didn't fit within program guidelines. We brainstormed possibilities and settled on one, to which I said, "Yes."

I don't think I will ever again be as narrow in my approach to understanding what learning is, what teaching is, what compassion and intelligence are, than I must have been early on at Castleton. Thank you, John Duval, for the power of YES!

1999

John Duval

I came upon this writing about John. I can hardly speak. He is dead, throat cancer. I remember so much: his final exam on "quality"; his license plate "EDUCERE"; his hearty laugh and smiling eyes while exuding passion for new ideas, students' ideas, learning. I will always say yes, John; I will find a way to continue to honor the legacy you left behind. No doubt there are *many* Vermont educators who are doing exactly the same thing! You mattered.

2020

YES!

Where there is a will, a compassionate heart, an intelligent mind, then a YES can be found. It requires believe, and trust, and perhaps even work. Just all of it.

I am fairly sure I must have thought saying yes would require more of me than I wanted to give/make time for. (I didn't have my X word yet!) *Yes* can complicate things/require more effort than saying *No*. **No** ends the discussion, stops progress, shuts down thinking. So, **Yes** may *be* more difficult to say than **No**, but **Yes** is more often than not the better response. It really works!

1996

| Z | "zazz"

as in, Pizazz!

Find yours!!

Make Some!!!

Sparkle!!!!

2020

…I still believe…

    Hmm. I look at what I wrote in the 20th century and kind of half smile, half chuckle. Maybe I was just happy to be finished with my alphabet. Or maybe, just maybe, I was thinking that learning is a celebration of all that is and all that is possible. We see evidence of learning around us, every day. We see what human beings can conceive, invent, figure out, build, sing, plant, grow, dance, write, paint, draw, construct, consider, or theorize. Maybe I was just expressing what we all feel when we have accomplished something, when we have completed a task, when we can put it down and move ahead to something else. Maybe I was just confirming in my *own* mind how glad I was to have had a learning-teaching career. Maybe I was just encouraging myself to keep trying.

    Products, accomplishments, and actions are only momentary stopping points in our lives. The true celebration of learning is that we *can* learn. In our ways, in our time, as we are so able. Yes. We. Can!

~ THE END ~

Cheers to your learning lives and those of your students!

With *respect* and *sympathy*,

Judy   4. 17. 20

References

The authors mentioned in this book are located on the pages *italicized* following their name. *If no particular book is mentioned in the body of the text*, I offer at least one of their publications should you like to find it.

Eisner, Elliot. *p. 22.*
    (1994). (3rd Ed.). *The educational imagination: On the design and evaluation of school programs.* New York: MacMillan.

Finkel, Donald L. *p. 42.*
    (2000). *Teaching with your mouth shut.* Portsmouth, NH: Boynton/Cook Pub., Inc.

Kuhn, Deanna. *pp. 31, 35, 42, 58.*
    (2005). *Education for thinking.* Cambridge, Mass: Harvard University Press.

Langer, Ellen J. *pp. 42, 58.*
    (1997). *The power of mindful learning.* Reading, Mass: Addison-Wesley.

Noddings, Nel. *p. 13.*
    (1984). *Caring: A feminine approach to ethics and moral education.* Berkeley: U. of California Press.
    (1992). *The challenge to care in schools.* NY: Teachers College Press.

Postman, Neil. *p. 32, 42.*
    (1995). *The end of education: Redefining the value of school.* NY: Vintage Books/Random House.

Tillich, Paul. *p. 41.*
    (1952). *The courage to be.* New Haven, CT: Yale University Press.

Warner, Sylvia-Ashton. *p. 9, 10.*
    (1963). *Teacher.* NY: Simon and Schuster.

Wulf, Andrea. *p. 43.*
    (2015). *The invention of nature: Alexander von Humboldt's new world.* NY: Alfred A. Knopf.